Look Again

Commentary
on The
23rd Psalms

William Thompson Jr.

Preface ~ Commentary to the 23rd Psalms

A comparative comprehensive study on the wording and the meaning of the message of the 23rd Number of the Psalms...................

I am of the opinion, that as result of pure laziness relative to prayer and outright refusal to believe that the bible is true; there is too much interpretation, and not enough revelation of the scripture received from the Holy Spirit; in the hearts of people worldwide.

The biblical interpreters have taken it upon themselves to say what they think that the bible intends to say to us, they are answering question that have never even been asked; and they often give suggested opinionated reasons for that in which there is no reasonable neither unreasonable conjecture in the dialogue of the scripture.

Many people of the world are saying that Modern Religion separates people rather than binding us all together; although it is no excuse for them to stay away from God; and the bible. They are determined to reestablish the validity of scripture based authority for governing the behavior of modern man.

God; nor the scripture; are at all accepted as having the power in these present times to govern the behavior of mankind. People feel that they have outgrown the authority of the scripture, they feel that life has been given to them to live as they are pleased to do so!

An invisible God and an invisible authority of the scripture are too intangible to have a hand in the governing guardianship of the individual livelihood of people who have such dreadfully painful circumstances of living on a daily basis; some would think anyway? It is no wonder that so many people are determined not to believe; neither to obey the scripture; as a result of having had them so theologically disected and unapollogetically tampered with by collegiate secular authority, who obviously have no spiritual connection to God in Christ

Preface

Jesus.

The human mind, though it is very powerful and a necessary tool for mentally digesting important information and corresponding accordingly to the presentation, it is but yet finite and not quite dictatorial enough to define and or to redefine the actual infinite intentions of God's eternal meaning of the scripture. He made the minds that we of all walks of life, are enabled to think.

No class room nor internet teaching/learning institution have the ability to get inside of the mind of God, to inner-comprehend the will of God outside of the Holy Ghost. Absoluttely no one is ever allowed to teach and to instruct other upcoming instructors and teachers, giving validation to doubt or to discredit the infallible written word of God.

People nowadays have way too much advice to give on the word of God, who have never been made authoritative to give any such advice through the power of the Holy Ghost. As of late, people began to step forward as authority figures of the bible having never been called upon by God to do so, because they desired to have their own say on the scripture.

Those people seemed to have a great audiences of spiritually inquisitive as well as very religiously gullible people of equal proportions who are indeed willing to be told what they ought to think of the scripture. Whether or not people really intellectually internalized what they heard relative to what these speakers had to say for the sake of embracing the information that they released; they did give ear to such unqualified voices of the scripture.

Of the most dangerous elements of the disqualified voices who handled the scriptures; those who listened to them often verbalized that their particular spin on the scripture made since to them! According to the scripture; Romans 10:7-14; teaches us that hearing the scripture by the aid of the sent preacher produces faith for all of them that hear the anointed spoken word of God.

As it is, many are listening while never actually hearing the message in the word of God. II Peter 1:5-9; talks to us about adding to our faith of which will bring the scripture, faith, and faith of the scripture

into much clearer comprehensive understanding of what the Father is saying to us through His own word!

So many others here in our free world of thought, have determined that we needed to hear the scripture from a more expanded perspective; or that we should just totally disregard the authenticity of the scripture altogether. Some who think themselves to be the authority of the scripture, their determination to re-interpret the scripture was not just for the sake of language dialect and dialogue of the scripture, but for the sake of loosening the authoritative yoke of behavorial control, necessary for everyone who professes to believe that the God of the scripture is indeed real and true.

Looking into the added interpretations; it became aware to me that people desired to read the bible without being obligated to believe anything that they had read in the scripture. Neither do they desire to be held accountable for knowing the truth of the scripture concerning relative to maintaining biblical lifestyles that are not convenient in societies of suggested freestyle living according to individual choice, having to answer to no one! In their own minds they might have thought that they were making it more desirable to receive God on their own interpretive accounts?

All I know is that God; is God all by Himself; He doesn't need any of our help to be all that He IS; being God! [Hebrews 11:6 ~ *But without faith it is impossible to please him: for he that cometh to God must believe that He is, and that He is a rewarder to them that diligently seek Him.*] God; is God!

So, of the 23rd Psalms; it has become so much more easily digestible for the readers to read, hear, and to receive that God is basically the best slot machine ever. You give the very least, and be assured the He the Lord God will pump out the very most to you? Well let's explore the meaning of the scripture for the sake of making faith more attainable to the presence and the awesome benefits of God's ability given to mankind. We will see the manifested power of God's blessings as result of obedience and a trusted relationship between us and our God, through His word :...................

Let's just examine a few of the interpretive versions of the scripture, Psalms 23 in its entirety in three different biblical versions all of

Preface

the English translations, since the King James Version......

Contemporary English Version ~

Psalms 23....................

1.You, Lord are my shepherd. I will never be in need. 2. You let me rest in fields of green grass. You lead me to streams of peaceful water, and refresh my life. 3. You are true to your name, and you lead me along the right paths. 4. I will walk through valleys as dark as death, but I won't be afraid. You are with me, and your shepherd's rod makes me feel safe. 5. You treat me to a feast, while my enemies watch. You honor me as your guest, and you fill my cup until it overflows. 6. Your kindness and love will always be with me each day of my life, and I will live in your house, Lord.

The Living Bible

Because the Lord is my shepherd, I have everything I need! 2-3. He lets me rest in the meadow grass and he leads me beside the quiet streams. He gives me new strength. He helps me do what honors him the most. 4. Even when walking through the dark valley of death will not be afraid, for you are close beside me, guarding, guiding all the way. 5. You provide delicious food for me in the presence of my enemies. You have welcomed me as your guest, blessing overflow! 6. Your good and unfailing kindness shall be with me all of my life, and afterwards I will live forever in your home.

Wycliffe Bible

The Lord governeth me, and nothing shall fail me. (and there is nothing that I shall lack.) 2. In the place of pasture there he hath set me. He nourished me on the water of refreshing; (he hath set me in a place of pasture. He nourished me by the waters of refreshing.) 3. He converted my soul. He led me forth on the paths of righteousness; for his name. (he transformed my soul. He led me forth on the paths of righteousness/on the right paths; for the sake of his name.) 4. For why though I shall go in the midst of shadow of death; I shall not dread evils, for thou art with me. Thy rod and thy staff; those have comforted me. (for though I go in the midst of the shadow of death, I shall fear no evil; for thou art with me. Thy rod and thy staff, they have comforted me.) 5. Thou hast made ready a board in my sight; against them that trouble me. Thou hast made fat mine head with oil; and my cup, that filleth greatly, is full clear. (Thou hast prepared a table before me; before those who trouble me. Thou hast covered my head with oil; and my cup, which thou greatly filleth, is full, indeed it runneth

over.) 6. And thy mercy shall follow me; in all the days of my life. And that I dwell in the house of the Lord; into the length of days. (And thy love shall follow me; all the days of my life. And I shall live in the house of the Lord forever and ever.)

 **Look Again**

1. The "Lord;" [is] ~ the eternally existent master of the universal cosmos; the maker and the creator of the Heavens and the earth, and all that are therein……….

My shepherd, ~ my protector; my provider; and my guide; followed and unquestioned as He leads me from day to day……….

I shall not want. ~ I will never exercise my own personal will against His will for me; nor will I exalt my desires for me above His desires for my life……

2. He maketh me to lie down in green pastures: ~ simply put; He gives me Life, with the intent to instruct me how to live. He knows that he has given me purpose and validated reasoning for being here on the face of the planet; so as a result; whatever he requires me to do; it behooves me to obey Him………….. He is forever responsible for the fact that I am positioned where living flourishes with increase and plenteous prosperity.

He leadeth me beside the still waters. ~ He leads me to the place of peaceful tranquility where troubles are commanded to be seated and to come to a complete rest; that is if and when I follow His leading for me; Romans 8:14…….. [Isaiah 26:3]

3. He restoreth my soul: ~ He brings me back into the control of my emotions when I will have lost it; whenever I turn to him, or even turn back to him, he has the remedy for the flail emotions that I have allowed to run my own imagination at times, wildly out of control…….. He picks me up from the ground when I am fallen, and He puts me back where I belong even as if I had never fallen.

He leadeth me in the paths of righteousness for His names sake. ~ because I reside under the power of His name; knowing that I can't find the path of righteousness and walk therein all by myself, He's there to show

Preface

me the way, and to submerge me into the way of His righteousness, because of His eternally exalted name…………..

4. *Yea though I walk through the valley of the shadow of death,* ~ we that are alive are sure to die; when our loved ones are separated from us in death, and even in those times when death is all around us as a result of major disasters, earthquakes, tsunamis, hurricanes, tornados, wars, sicknesses, diseases and whatever may be the cause, they are all the realities of the lowest painful moments of living here on the earth and of the greater causes of death…………..

I will fear no evil: ~ no need to lose heart nor confidence in the power of God, never to lose sight on the fact that God is with me to keep me and to protect me from the evil of this world, feeling as if there is no help for me……….. As sure as there is God; there is hope.

For thou art with me; ~ God you are ever present with me, at all times…

Thy rod and thy staff they comfort me. ~ You correct me and comfort me whenever I need it most………………..

5. *Thou preparest a table before in the presence of my enemies:* ~ no one can truly prevent me from what you have for me; knowing that you do not always knock my enemies down, as there are those times when your desire for me is to lift me up instead, to be seen of my enemies that the way for me had already been completed, citing the fact that there is nothing that could ever be done successfully to stop me from finishing my purpose and reaching my goals in this life; though at time they may hinder my progress…….

Thou anointest my head with oil; ~ you have empowered me with the endowment of true son-ship to penetrate the ways of man that they may know you in the power of your resurrection and the fellowship of your sufferings, being made conformable unto the death of the cross……….

My cup runneth over. ~ I am full of your grace and your spirit and Love even beyond my ability to totally comprehend it; it's bubbling over in me and flowing out of me…………………….

6. *Surely goodness and mercy shall follow me all the days of my life:* ~ thank God that you will not hold my true character against me from before

the time that I met you and came to know you as my savior and my Lord; the promises to them that love you will never be forgotten concerning my life, I can rest in joy and the assurance that Jesus paid it all for me, and that the design of his mission in the earth was and is all finished for me; the best is even yet to come! Better things ahead...........

And I will dwell in the house of the Lord forever. ~ the ultimate promise to us here in this life that we are living on earth, is that even in our earthly reign we live faithfully surrounded by all that is God; and all that is pertaining to God; to the very end, we will live with the Father in heaven. But; it also means that we are enhoused in the presence of the Father's spirit while here on the earth in the presence of other mere men of the flesh. He promises never to leave us neither to forsake us................

Copyright 2016

By; *William Thompson, Jr.*

PUBLISHED BY

Write Everlasting Tips,

Publishing company

Printed in the United States of America

ISBN -0-9755994-3-7

ISBN 978-0-9755994-3-3

To contact the author, write

Write Everlasting Tips Publishing Co.

7525 Arbor Hill Dr.

Fort Worth, Texas 76120

Unless otherwise indicated, all Scripture

quotations are from the King James Version

of the Bible.

All rights reserved. Written permission must be secured from the publisher to use or reproduce any part of this book, except for brief quotations embodied in church related publications, critical review or articles.

About the Author

Born March 12, 1961 in El'paso, Texas, to the union of the late Rev. William Thompson Sr. & Rev. Daisy Y. Mclawler-Thompson; the family later relocated to Fort Worth, Texas in 1967 where he grew up in the church singing in the choir, learning to study his own bible, and participating in all of the youth activities faithfully.

He attended the Fort Worth Independent School District; graduated from P. L. Dunbar Sr. High, class of 79'. He was an honor student although he did not graduate with honors; his very best subjects where he excelled were English and Math. He was a Member of the Marching Band; Concert Band; Stage Band; School Chorus; his senior year he was the star of the Senior Play; "Roll Me Out To Sea" where he sang and played the piano. He was an initiator of the very first Dunbar Gospel Choir and musician; an after school project.

He attended Tarrant County Junior Colledge 1980, Vogue Bueaty Colledge 1981, and Dallas Theological Seminary 1986. Has spent the bulk of his time in coporate worship studies; multiple siminars on ministry, church ediquate, bible studies, music seminars for worship, revivals, conferences- pastoral, prayer, laymen, and of couse many conferences that cater to the total man.

He has been a partaker in several activities and auxilaries. Most of all he has been a servant to the body of Christ. An avid worker and a giver to the church unselfishly. He thoroughly operates impeccible as an anointed Prophet of God; whereas he has ministered to many people in the Kingdom of God across the country, and over the phone in India, Africa, and London. He is known and respected as a "True Prophet" of God.

He has been ministering the gospel since Feb. 7, 1982, and has engaged in studies and training of the bible. He has been in the church all of his natural life and has the experience of a faithful churchman which lends the passion for which he ministers the gospel of God. He has been ordained since June 1998.

By the age of 3 years he had already began to express a passion to play the piano and to preach the Gospel. He is a talented instumentalist, and has composed many songs. He has ministered in music for ministries in the DFW Metro-plex, and OKC, OK. He has traveled with evangelist, and has been the guest musician for many revivals, musicals, weddings, conferences, recordings and etc.

His uncle; the Late Apostle Russell Thompson, laid his hand on him at the age of 11, from that point on he knew that there was more for him in the Lord. He moved to the next level of worship in an effort to get to that which he desired most of the Lord. Pastor Thompson has crossed the lines of denominational affiliations as a friend and brother, enabling him to be identified as a child of God and not Just a Baptist, a Methodist, a Pentecostal, or for that matter, just another member of the Church Of God In Christ!

He founded and pastored the Tried Whole Truth Foundation Ministry; in Fort Worth, Texas; As instructed by the Lord he later changed the name to The Spoken Word Center where he had 8 [1998-2005] years of successful ministry under both the names. Souls were indeed saved, people were filled with the Holy Ghost; we observed miracles of healing and deliverance; demons cast out; lives changed and many ministries were realized and answered to the call of God.

He founded and established the Spoken Word Center, School of Prophetic Excellence 2003. As of late as we are re-launching the ministry, we have again changed the name of the ministry to The Kingdom Impact Certen of the Spoken Word Church, Int. We have been instrumental in working with and for several different ministries since as of late 2005 until 2014. We have been commissioned to go on forward full force with the ministry of the Kingdom Impact Center of the Spoken Word Church.

He has since preached many revivals where deliverance and the manifested presence of the Lord are witnessed. He has become an avid teacher to those who are new to the body of Christ, instructing them to know and to practice the presence of God in pure worship and praise to our God; in Christ Jesus. He is a real true lover of people; especially to those who are of the household of faith across the board; if you can love him, and even if you can't, he's committed to loving you.

By the grace of God and divine providence, he found his way back to the grass roots of his own spiritual inheritance. Pastor Thompson hails from an extensive linage of dedicated ministers. He's a decendant of the Late; Reverend Vol William McLawler of Louisville, Kentucky; and of the first generation Church of God In Christ East Texas; have been active in Texas Northeast 1st Jurisdiction under the now late Prelate J. N. Haynes where he worked in the District; State; and the National music departments.

His endeavor is to serve the people of the Lord everywhere that will receive of the awesome gift of the Holy Ghost to which he has been endowed. Pastor Thompson has been married to Sharon Renee for 32 years and is the father of Three children.

Dedication

In response to the revelation that you gave to me over 25 years ago; I obediently penned these revelations for the benefit of the ministers of the gospel of Jesus Christ. I give these truths to those who have an ear to hear what the spirit have to say to the church; that can indeed hear!

Finally: this work is dedicated to my own matured family who have been with me through all of the writing of the books that God has given me to write; they must know and believe that I love them dearly for all of their support.

Sharon Rene Thompson ~ Misty My'Chelle ~ Aaron Lamond ~William III......... You're The Best*****

Mother Daisy M. Thompson; and to all of the Thompson's

I Love You All

Table of Contents

Preface	1
Dedication	XII
Introduction	XIV

Verse One --- 23
    I'm His; The Lord Is Mine!

Verse Two -- 37
    I Hear; I Obey!

Verse Three --- 57
    I'm Restored To Follow!

Verse Four --- 77
    I Walk; With God! No Fear; I'm Safe!

Verse Five -- 99
    Table"s Set; I'm Spirit Filled!

VerseSix --- 129
    For Sure; Lord I'm In Here!

Conclusion -- 151

Conclusion

Introduction

*I*ntroduction

As we embark on the biblical accounts of David; it is our endeavor to reexamine the meaningful relevance and the intended relativism associative for us in todays time, applicable for our daily affairs in relationship with the Father in Heaven. The story of this shepherd boy is not just for our entertainment and enjoyment of reading; as some might have you to think of it as being. We are given the formula through praise and worship to receive and to maintain God's richest blessings for our lives.

There is no mention of David being raised in the schools of ministry of his own times, or the priesthood where he would have been in training for worship or for temple ministry? But somehow through his dedication and skill he was known and recognized as an anointed cunning player upon his instrument/s; so much so that when such a cunning player was indeed required, David's name was brought to the forefront being recommended as the best at his time. [1 Samuel 16:18]

We realize that he was a very skilled musician and a powerfully anointed Psalmist; as it was also reported that the Lord was with him! We might be led to think that there had to have been some form of training in his adolescence upbringing that would award him such maneuverability in the ministry of music and worship? The people of his own contemporary times remembered him as being one who truly was acquainted with the Father in Heaven.

It is the common spiritual deception of many, to even most people past and present; of biblical explorative studies to believe it to be impossible that he would have a word of encouragement, instruction, or any reasonable declarative guidelines relative to worship for his own generation and for all of the future generations to follow, being that he had been put out to the pasture on the backside of the wilderness, in seclusion tending unto the sheep, rather than

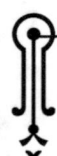

Psalms Twenty ~ Three

to have been placed on the platform in the temple of the synagogue?

This psycho analysis of theoretical reasoning is simply because we have often either overlooked or totally disregarded the glorious benefit of this shepherd boy, in that he had been alone with God out in the field worshiping and glorifying God as he tended unto the sheep. The average so-called believer who attend services at the churches often fail to worship God in the spirit and in truth, therefore in my own opinion, they are often clueless to any such benefits of worshipping and praising God. As result of willful worshipping and praising God; God revealed the greater benefiting mysteries of worship and praise to this little lad.

It is possible that so many people arrive at this particular dissertation as a result of the lack of understanding and failure to believe that God could endow the life of such an one who has never been instructed in the word and the doctrine of God by men of leadership stature and acclaim; such as to the likeness of pastors and seeminary instructors, and even the Sunday school and bible school teachers in their churches; anyway my friend God can, and God did indeed endow David!

"David", the youngest son of Jesse, the Ruddy little lad; out in the field tending to his father's sheep; he is the topic of discussion in this particular dialogue of study. He is the last and the final son of Jesse to be looked upon and later anointed king by the most endowed prophet Samuel; [1 Samuel 16:11-13] for certain God had sent the Prophet Samuel on a mission to find the replacement of the Kingdom headship, seeing that the Lord had rent the kingdom out of the hands of King Saul.[1 Samuel 16:1]

Many may choose to see David as the naughty little trouble making kid who could not be trusted to behave himself wisely or to do any other job that might have been among everybody else, so he was sent away from the fellowship of the people to go and tend to the sheep outback in the wilderness, or out in the field alone. For a truth; he was all by himself with the sheep in the field as it relates to having no other physical contact with people, but mind you; he was never left alone without protection and comfort, as the Lord was with him at all times.

The youthful inquisitiveness of most young men made it impossible for them to be left alone with the sheep out in the pasture; as many were

Introduction

tempted to experiment with the sheep knowing that the female sheep's sexual organs were exact to that of the woman; ungodly fact of history but true; of which is another topic of interest to be explored at another time. Love for God and true worship keeps the mind clear of naughty inquisitions that don't please the Lord. Note: it will also keep the body from indulging into sinful practices that will condemn the soul and cause the judgement of the word and the spirit of God to be enacted against the sinful behavior.

In this very carnal mined, unbelieving, and negative thinking generation of people who are full of Hollywood's depiction of most everything that we read in the bible, some might be quick to believe that the filmmaker John Hughes; who wrote the movie "Home Alone" starring "Macauley Culkin"; might have been giving his own interpretative dictum of the "Shepherd Boy" haven been left at home alone, although David was never left at home alone, he was alone with the sheep; though in the presence of God.

John Hughes, exposes the vulnerabilities of the lonely lonesome child at home all alone to deal with the cracks and the creeks of the house as the winds howl against it, and the squeaks and shrills of the opening doors as the doors move on its hinges in need of being oiled; he even shows how the boys mind might have been fearfully stretched into many different imaginative directions.

But, what his creative mind could not show you through a Hollywood film; would be the brilliant supernatural relationship between David and the God of all the ages. David worshipped until God said that; "David, *was a man after mine own heart*"; as this kind of worshipful reverence to our God doesn't often find its way into the heart of mere men who could never wrap their carnal minds filled with selfish motives and concerns, around the reality of dancing themselves into the realm of the spirit losing sight of the pressing daily affairs upon us, that cause us stress and worry. True worship to our God is the remedy to the stresses of life and worry. God Loves Us!

Through the aid of reading the scripture, it is evident to me that all of the host of heaven were opened up unto David even at his very young and tender age, even before he could be declared an adult responsible for his own life. There is a definite spiritual danger in leaving a child alone to think and to mentally explore all by themselves depending on where the child has been left

Psalms Twenty ~ Three

alone to themselves; but in the case of David; on the other hand it later proved to be a very benefitial.

There is never a time that a human being, once haven been born upon the face of the earth, that they are not the spiritual target of our Lord; and or of Satan! Leaving them alone suggests unprotection and the lack of spiritual covering to watch over them to ensure that they are never negatively infiltrated, unless leaving them means that you have turned them over into the presence of the Lord; or to the award of the state?

Reflect with me for a moment; the Prophet Samuel; who anoints this young lad to be the king over all of Israel and Judah; it was indeed he himself; whose mother left him in the care of the High Priest Eli, in the temple. His mother Hannah gave him back to the Lord as she had promised to do so. [1 Samuel 1:11] The paralleled mystery of these two young lads, lies within how that they were both chosen and used of God greatly as a result of haven been set aside and trained to worship and to know the presence of God and the powerful expression of His own voice speaking to them even at an early age.

As we have searched the scripture, it's apparent to us that there had to have been something very special about the shepherd boy, that never allowed his father or his brothers to fear for his wellbeing out in the field tending to the sheep. I'm sure that the boy showed signs of independence and assurance whereas he could definitely handle the sheep and any predator that would threaten the wellbeing of the sheep; perhaps he could fight? He had awesome footwork in that he was swift on his feet and he must have been quick and skilled with his hands? He showed signs of having great agility!

As a matter of the fact we know that David was skilled with his hands as a musician; and according to accounts of the scripture, he was knowledgeable of choosing rocks that would be quickly propelled as he knew how to skillfully shoot those rocks into the atmosphere, much faster than any enemy could move in his direction to ever get to him. In the face of many obstacles David prevailed and lived to carry out his ultimate purpose and assignment in his life. No adversary was ever successful at taking David out from his youth up! He always prevailed because the Lord was with him………………….

The picture of David gleaned from the scripture does not show us an indigent naughty little boy who meddled in others business matters to which

Introduction

he should not have; rather it shows us an inquisitive young lad who was determined to know God in the fullness of His eternal power and God-head. David tended to his father's sheep, which means that he paid attention to the sheep as he kept watch over them, which allows us to realize that David often minded his own business! No one could ever be successful minding the business of everyone else' other than their own, as things often swiftly get out of control and out of whack.

Neither David's father nor his brothers would have allowed him to remain in the field with the sheep had he been incapable of keeping them safe from hurt harm and danger. I get the feeling often that they were rather over-protective of David as the younger sibling and instructive to him as a parent or guardian would rule over a child. Being alone in the field doesn't mean that he was given the freedom to roam freely as he wished to do so; David had guidance and guidelines for which he obediently followed.

We do see a young boy who purposefully wondered into areas of worship that many even to this very day would never dare to even explore. This is more than evident to us as we read the declarative words of David saying to us that "THE LORD IS;" explorative worship reveals such to any individual who dare to know God in the entire expression of His person. The truth is that all of the spiritual accounts of David were not, and could not be written in the scripture. There is no telling of the many angelic visits, of the spiritual transformations that he might have experienced out in the field while tending to the sheep.

We do read in I SAMUEL; where God tells Samuel that David was a man after His own heart, which tells me that David spent his time seeking ways to please the Lord, to the point that he would be able to know those things about God that would be obscure to the average man on the face of the earth. As a result of his ability to worship God going beyond the realm of understanding his own human reasoning; he was chosen by God.

I am of the opinion that we are not yet been made fully aware of the meaningful dialogue in the 23rd number of the Psalms. In general we bask in a designated proposed theorem, although, it is but however, a very nominally invisionment acceptance of the scripture that we are admonished to follow, purposefully avoiding the true colloquial comprehension of the writer's mes-

Psalms Twenty ~ Three

sage, so as to soften the blow from the pen to the purpose of the words written. So as inspired of the Holy Spirit, we will explore in amplified detail the outlaid and the outlined message of the 23rd Psalms..................

We as human beings in general are grossly slanted and a bit twisted in our understanding of what should be our relationship with the Father in Heaven; as a result of the purposeful lob-sided denominational reading perception, which suggest to us that the Father has but to do everything all by Himself, in an effort to make the relationship between us work to the fullest potential, which is total deception!

It is true however; that "GOD" is all that and then some! But, we likewise also have been fearfully and wonderfully made and created by God; to do our part to make the relationship flourish, measure up and mature to the potential of the Father's capacity, desired for us all. Our God is all wise and all knowing, no one could ever know better than He, that we could never please Him without haven been made initially capable to do so from the very beginning. Even as an automobile maker knows what it will take to get the very best optimum performance from the automobile that they have designed and manufactured in the factory.

The 23rd number of the Psalms is the most quoted; misquoted; though the most in-comprehended written number of the Psalms in the bible. Everybody runs to grab the 23rd Psalms for almost every emotional experience; whenever they get in trouble, or whenever they lose a loved one in death, and whenever they are in fear for any reason; this is the word of the scripture that a great number of the people seem to believe is available to reassure any people for any reason, of which my friend is simply gross negligence of the scripture. Under these circumstances, the word of God is held in unrighteousness and totally embraced out of context to the actual meaningful relevance of its truest definition. [Romans 1: 18]

The sad commentary after reviewing what I have been given to write is that most people are not going to hear that they are in error misquoting the scripture out of context to its truest meaningful relevance to our daily lives. The scripture already has its established installed meaning that is applicable to be implicated into the living activity of all who are actively living upon the face of the earth, whether they are people of the church or of the secular society.

Introduction

You will also find that the scripture is well balanced and well-founded upon the truth of God; which is what enables it to meet the need of all who would refer to the scripture for all the benefit of living. You will also note that God is neither Santa Clause nor a slot machine available to pump out our most immediate request like a genie in a bottle. The given designation of the 23rd number of the Psalms is all but the same in description! Although most of us, we do understand that God is our provider and the source of all of our supply, however a greater percentage of us will fail to reason in the understanding of our minds, as to why it is that He will do so for us, only at His own will and discretion.

We don't tell God what to do and when to do it; we simply ask in faith for those things that are according to the Lord's will for our lives, for our good, but, for His purpose, [Romans 8:28]. There is simply no way that we could ever be in full operation of faith, as we simultaneously doubt the truth of God in Christ Jesus. What need would there be; for any of us to ask in faith if God was just going to do whatever we ever wanted or ever needed without any participation on our part?

The plants that you want to grow don't just grow out of the ground on your thoughts alone. You have to cultivate the earth and plant the proper seed for the intended crop; of which after doing so, you then have got to water the seed in the ground and even after you begin to witness the growth of the plant you have still got to water the crop until it has matured to the point that you are able to receive the fruit thereof.

It is my endeavor that all readers of this written commentary come to the place of total comprehension and the ability to put forth the energy and effort to be all that God is calling for us to be in this present world. This should be a joyful experience to hear with me the voice of God and to feel the breath of God as He breathes upon these words of wisdom to show us the total picture of His will for our lives. It is the Lord's will and desire that we as a people of faith and love live to the full potential of our faith in God.

Come on now and journey with me on this explorative expedition; there is a word of clarity and definition just for you my friend. God desires for you to know Him just as deeply intimate and as sincerely pure as you may desire to know Him! Come on let's see; let's look again at what the spirit has to say unto the church through this written commentary............................

Can You See Now?

William Thompson Jr. 2017

Verse One

"Comentary on The 23rd Psalms"

I'm His; The Lord Is Mine!

The Lord is my shepherd, I shall not want. [Psalms 23:1]

"The Lord; Is;"

Unlike many of us today, David put more than his head; or his mind and maybe his bodily presence into the matter of knowing God; he came forth with the intimate intention of getting acquainted with God; with his whole heart, his soul and his total being.

I'm reminded in the scripture that David made himself acquainted with the Lord and went forward to worship Him as the Lord God that He is!

David made sure that he, himself; loved the Lord before ever trying to do that which brings recognition to the name of the Lord of Host. It is very wise to know the Lord before attempting to answer the call of the Lord to go forth and to preach the word; seeking to make a name for yourself.

Firstly; David said; "The Lord;" [Isaiah 53:], acknowledging that being God; in every expression of His Deity and His reigning reality as the creator; He is The Almighty!

He's the Greatest Supreme personality in all of Heaven and Earth; superior to humanity, but available to hear and to answer our prayers according to His will for us.

The Lord; really does have eyes that see us and ears that hear us, a

mouth to speak to us and arms to hold us and to reach out to us; and finally the Lord has hands with which to touch us.[Isaiah 59:1]

However, let it be known of you that there is nothing at all natural or physical about the characteristics of God; He is spirit! [St. John 4:24]

Whenever God needed a physical touch of Himself in the earth, He sent to us Jesus the Christ; son of the living God; however mere men refused to touch Him, other than to crucify Him, in the earth!

The greater percentile of human beings failed to embrace {Emanuel} ~ not understanding the He is God with us. He was indeed present in the flesh; the natural form of mankind in the earth. But unlike David, men refused to see as He is!

It's better to worship God in the spirit and in truth thus becoming a worshipper yourselves before attempting to be the worship leader! It's taken too long for so many to get the understanding that salvation must precede being a suitable workman in the ministry of God!

It's as simple as that! It is necessary that we tell the Lord Yes, and mean yes to His will! We need not to attempt to influence God to say yes to our own will and desires instead.

The wrong idea is that we can come forth and do the things for the Lord that we may in fact desire to do on our own inner drives, having never been called on by the Lord, to do those things.

Doing stuff for God; does not at all bespeak of our dedication and neither of our Love for who He; the Lord; is indeed! At best it simply states that you're determined to do some stuff in the local church; but unchecked in the spirit of your mind?

Your reasoning and your motives are all off, never having been change and washed in the blood of the Lamb of God. Your mind still belongs to you and to Satan!

This truth has been spoken on many occasions, but so many refuse to hear! They're determined to prove that they know better than the preacher about doing things for God.

They would much rather believe and embrace within themselves that God knows that they are doing a favor for Him, and that God appreciativem to them for doing so; despite of hearing the word of the scripture preached.

Some of the messages that have been preached over the pulpit in the churches have gone the wrong direction in the spirits of many of the hearers; sermons to the likes of saying that no one can do the things of which you have been called upon to do in the same manner of which you do them; which is the truth, whether you are good at what you do or not so good at all.

But, so many people hear the message saying to them that God indeed need them; as if to suggest that the Kingdom of God will suffer lack and be in great danger of failure without them?

So my questions to any of you that think like this; exactly what did God do before you came on the scene?

Might it also have been too late for the Kingdom of God if you were so desperately needed before you got here?

Since you're here, what difference has it made, and how obvious has it been to the rest of the body of Christ that your piece of the puzzle had been out of place?

David exemplified supernatural authority and power while tending to his father's sheep out in the field. As a result, whenever David met Goliath of Gath; out on the battle field, he was well prepared and equipped for such the unusual battle presented by this giant.

In his own personal time with the Lord he was able to tap into the power source of God's anointing.

Alike David, many have had spiritual transitions and transmissions into the spirit realm though yet alive and living out their own natural human experience! There are some things of the spirit of the Lord that you are not going to be blessed to receive except that you spend personal time with the Lord.

There are places of the spirit that we are able to travel to on the established transmission of praise and worship.

While such a statement as this may appear to be a bit incredulous to some, others have had the experience of what might be described as outer body experiences.

It is going to be necessary for you to be spiritually informed and well acquainted with the authority and the power of the spirit of the Lord, if in fact you're going to be successful going forward in the will of the Lord for your life in ministry.

All that we are able to see with our naked eyeballs does not bespeak of everything that there is to ever see; as there is so much more to be seen in the realm of the spirit.

Could we who are now ourselves worshippers; ever imagine where David might have ventured spiritually into the realistic realm of

God's presence, being in the fields with the sheep, out there all alone with no prohibitions to prevent him from entering into the spirit realm?

Worship is where we realize the truest benefits of living close to the Lord. I'm talking about spending that personal time with the Lord when we are all alone in the presence with the Lord, whereas we glorify the Lord for who He is, not asking for anything personal, or being selfish in prayer.

Worship; is the place and the time that we are allowed to ask God the deeper more intricate things of the spirit and get the detailed answers that we will never forget, ever; it's called revelation!

It's the time and the place of spiritual manifestation, whereas angelic beings may walk up in your presence and talk with you, or manifest themselves to you and reveal the glorious splendor of their own created beings.

David; saw some things that intrigued him to go on deeper into the worship of the Lord, whereas God downloaded a power to him that would defeat every challenge presented to him.

The truth is that most people don't have a real clue as pertaining to what real true worship is. Most simply believe that whenever we go to the church for a service to complete corporate worship, that they have satisfied all prequisites of worship.

Worship speaks what we could never say to the Lord, and it raises question to the Lord that perhaps we had never even had the intellectual preparedness to verbally construct to Him? [Ephesians 3:20]

Worship allows us to travel paths to which our physical feet will never tread upon; we take hold of that to which our own hands will never be able to grasp and to manipulate.

True worship gives consent to the love that we have for God and the love that God has for us to be realized and examined upon the tables of our hearts.

Worship displays to the Lord that we really have surrendered to His will and to His plans for our lives. Worship acknowledges that we desire all that the Lord ever has for us, and that we are intent on having the greater things of God for our own possession.

So as David worshipped the Lord in the beauty of holiness, he was also made aware of the instructions and the guidelines for getting the things of the Lord done with total excellence and grace. David believed God!

Verse ~ One

You will never be a successful servant of the Lord doubting Him all of the way. Once David realized that God; is God; he reverenced Him as God and gave Him all of the glory and the praise, never allowing anything to come between him and his God; forever.

Secondly; David said; "THE LORD IS", he knew that there is none greater than the Lord, our God! He never approached any challenge as if to be lacking the power and or the authority to conquer the challenge or the challenger; he was confident and sure; but, he was confident in the Lord; sure of his God!

"THE LORD IS"- GIVES REFERENCE TO THE FACT THAT JESUS IS LORD AND MASTER OF THE UNIVERSE. IT BESPEAKS OF HIS SUPERIORITY AMONG ALL THAT ARE CALLED GODS AND THE MAGISTRATES WHO CLAIM TO BE THE MORE ELITE PEOPLE OF THE EARTH.

THIS STATEMENT BESPEAKS OF THE ACTIVITY OF GOD AMONG HIS PEOPLE IN THE EARTH; IT BESPEAKS OF WHAT THE LORD IS DOING FOR US, AND THROUGH US, AND OR EVEN WHAT THE LORD IS CAPABLE OF DOING THROUGHOUT ALL THE CREATED REALM OF HUMANITY IN ALL THE EARTH.

To say that the Lord is; makes the bold declaration that He is responsible for all that is! Time wouldn't be, the days of the week, the months of the year and on and on....

Everything that is in existence is given an explanation for being here whenever we simply say the Lord is……. He's responsible!

In reality we have not come to the point and the place of being able to say that we know the purpose for everything that has been placed on the face of the earth, but we do know that the Lord knows all that we are yet in question of, and He has all of the answers.

This statement is very familiar to us who are praisers and true worshippers of God; as we often find ourselves saying; {"The Lord Is"} blessing me right now!

While we reverence the almighty Lord of lords, and the King of kings; we recognize that there is none like Him in the Cosmos.

This statement establishes His superior dominance, and omnipotent reign as the almighty God, and the everlasting Father; the maker and the creator of the Heavens and the earth.

The Lord is in control and in consent of the living and the dead; there is never a time when the Lord

is not watchful of the living or the dead. I have said before and I will say it again; the dead would get up from their graves and live again if the Lord were not in control.

His decision to speak and the living suddenly die, or to speak and move his hand and a living being, leap into the womb of an appointed mother to give birth to the next living soul upon the earth; is all so because He is.

"My Shepherd"

David accepts the Lord as his own shepherd, and leader; as we often forget the fact that David; himself, was a shepherd boy tending to his own earthly father's sheep, we are also allowed to overlook the fact that he knew what it meant to assign the care of his own heavenly Father; as the shepherd and the watchman of his own soul.

The religious communities and the secular societies alike are so far gone on the idealism in the beliefs that the benefits of knowing God is all along the lines of being able to tell Him what to do, what we want and how those things ought to be done for us, and given to us.

This outrageously stretched imaginative focus of salvation being all get from God; and no give on our part; has affected the church to the point that it has become infected with this poisonous materialistic affirmation; now being passed on as if to be a direct message from the scripture.

Although there are benefits in serving the Lord, windows of access to the blessings of the Lord are opened unto us, as a result of the newly established relationship; but this doesn't mean that we are in control of how often or even how soon the benefits are released to us.

We are not given the authority to tell God what to do, and when to move from His throne to answer a request for us from the standpoint of being a ruler or a commander over God!

The greatest benefit of being saved is the blessing of knowing the Lord personally; having our sins pardoned and washed away, freeing us from the penalty of hell's eternal flame and torment.

Someone told someone else many years ago what they thought the word of God should mean, and the other person or persons accepted the teaching admonishment for truth; never ever having searched the scripture for themselves.

As a result, for generations now the story has been told in the manner that reflects the teachings from centuries past to all of the churches worldwide, at large.

Verse ~ One

Now it is rather difficult to teach the revealed significance of the scripture to the many masses of today for the sake of the padlocked acceptance of the foretold erroneous miss-teachings of the scripture.

David says; "The Lord is my Shepherd;" in his pristine acknowledgement of God, he declares that there is no one who could ever compare to our God, and he introduces the Lord as his leader and his guide, his ultimate provider and keeper.

Notice; David is not at all ashamed to reverence God as the all and all of his life, before his peers and to the ultimate counsel of his own diocese where he rules as king of the nation of Israel.

It is the job of the shepherd to feed the sheep by leading them to the pathway of the plenteous overflow of nourishment for the body, the soul, and the spirit of which God; the Lord has already previously provided.

David discovered that the Lord cared for the total man, in every aspect of living and of life. He found the Lord worthy of worshipful reverence, and all praise.

Before going forward with any of the other declarative statements of the Lord in the 23rd number of the Psalms; he emphatically establishes the recognizable deity and power of the Godhead!

I find it intriguingly introductive that David surrenders himself to the ownership of God; in my own way of speaking, David says to us that the Lord owns me!

When he had found that God; Himself; was and is greater than all mankind, and all that is created in the earth and the universe, he said; The Lord Is; and I like who He the Lord is; He hides me in the shelter of His arms, and He keeps me in the safety of His will for my life.

~ I surrender all to Him; He's My Shepherd!

He declares that God is his ruler and master, being the master and the ruler of the universe.

He wanted us to realize that God Himself is in control, only because he had come to realize that truth for himself as well![Psalms 27]

Too often we as people have a tendency to attempt at sharing truths, or at least purported truths that we ourselves have neither found the truths to be biblically sound and accurate, although the truths that we might have been introduce to might have been scripture from the holy bible, though haven been misrepresented and even seriously misinterpreted

out of the contextual, intended meaning of the scripture!

He; the great God; is responsible for everything that concerneth me, he's the metronome to the cadence of my stride, of the rhythm of the music in my head as I create melodies and songs of worship and adoration for the Lord; he is the all-knowing strategy of the fight down on the inside of me to defeat all of my enemies!

Being often separated from his family for the sake of caring for the sheep, David accepts the Lord as his Father; ultimate family and the head of his life, and the source of all of his supply. [Psalms 119:170]

He had come to know that God knows better than he did himself, what was best for him. It is paramount that we relent and back off from the helm of our daily affairs as being the leader of our lives, only inviting God in when things don't go as we had planned for them to.

Many people take off on a journey only to discover miles down the way after having traveled far away from home that they are on a journey that the Lord had never ordained for them to travel.

It would have been so much better had they acknowledged the Lord before ever taking off on the journey.]Proverbs 3:5-6]

The shepherd leads the sheep on the journey because he knows where the provisions have already been established for the sheep.

The compass, for the sake of knowing the direction of travel, is given to the shepherd and it is never given to the sheep that would never even knew how to read the compass.

A dedicated shepherd knows the location of where the sheep are presently presiding before they ever take to a journey to move out to another location for whatever the reason, which gives the shepherd the advantage of knowing which direction to go, in an effort to reach the given provisions.

Because sheep are often pursued as prey by many predators; the shepherd has to move the sheep from place to place, in an effort to shield and to protect the sheep from being the very next meal of any predator.

Also the grass will have been thoroughly devoured at a certain location; the sheep would starve to death should they remain in that particular space, so the shepherd leads them to more plenteous pastures of the Lord's provision.

Figuratively speaking; the messages in the pulpits of some

certain churches has been the very same since the inferrence of it's beginning! This is evidence that the grass have been long since before now devoured by the sheep.

The ministry itself is stagnant and in many aspects, it's dead! There is absolutely no growth of the people that attend that particular ministry; for the simple reason that there is no nourishment. They may be entertained, but it is for certin that they are not being fed!

David decided in his own heart that I will follow the Lord wherever He leads me, and I will receive whatever He provides for me, knowing that there is never going to be anything given by the Lord that would or could ever be distasteful and disgusting for me, and he knew that the Lord would never lead him in a desolate pathway of destruction.

It is so important that David get the message over to us that the Lord is the provider and just how wonderful it is. Many people have not as of yet surrendered to the leading of the Lord for their own lives as a result of being fearful that should they allow the Lord to be in control of their lives they are not going to be able to enjoy living as they would be pleased to do so?

All that the Lord provides is going to be as delightful as He is, being God! The Lord is sweet and good; always pleasant and peaceful.

The Lord is always as revitalizing as that breath of fresh air when breathing as if it were the very first breath that we had ever inhaled.

The Lord is as that very first refreshing drink of cold water to quench our thirst after being partched in the hot sun of the driest dessert without a canister of water for the journey.

He is as wonderful as the restoration of life at the very point of death! It is the plans of the enemy to cause every believer to disbelieve God, feeling that we had been given sub-care?

This is the reason that so many distasteful things have happened in our lives, the ultimate purposes for those things is to cause us to assign God as being responsible for allowing or for adding such hideous things to our lives, giving validated reasoning to be angry with God?

It may often feel that we had been given sour grapes and green persimmons causing our mouths to pucker being dried out and discomforted.

Everything opposite of the true character and spirit of God are often hurled right into the direct pathway of our thinking; as it is the

spirit of deception attempting to skew our true vision of God.

"I Shall Not Want"

In light of the divine recognition of just who God is in absolute identification, David goes on a step further to set himself in check, as he states; "I shall not want;" He declares in total surrender to the will of the Lord, I'm yours.

We can't be afraid of giving ourselves totally to the will of the Lord God for our lives! God always know what He's doing, especially whenever we don't know; He always knows what He is doing with you and me!

Let's never allow ourselves to talk about God as if He could ever blunder and make a mistake concerning us; He's too perfect to ever make a mistake!

WANT-{DESIRE-WILL} – TO WISH, TO CRAVE, TO HAVE A DEEP LONGING OR A YEARNING FOR SOMETHING OF A MATERIALISTIC PURPOSE OF SPIRIT, POSITION, OR OF NATURAL RESOURCES. NEEDS, ASPIRATIONS, DETERMINATION, AND OR EVEN SELF-CONTROL.......

David declares; "I SHALL NOT WANT!" While it have been determined that this verse of the scripture depicts that we can have whatever we want whenever we desire or request it; be it further resolved that we need desperately to look again into the deeper meanings of the scripture from David's perspective.

This scripture has been designated to mean that we have everything that we need, since the Lord is our shepherd? While there is some truth to this determination of the scripture; it is blown way out of context to what the true meaningful relationship with the Lord should reflect.

I have been the witness to observe that many of the truly believing and dedicated people of the Lord; that we all have those times in our walk with the Lord whereas we have to wait on the Lord for certain provisions to manifest.

There have been those times when we are simply tested and tried for the sake of the greater release of faith in the Lord.

We simply do not walk about this life having things to fall out of the sky to our possession, having never to ask of the Lord and then to wait for the things that we have asked for to come to us.

Whether we are obedient to the Lord's word and to His will according to the scripture, many have resolved to believe that God has to give to us whatever we want relative to His position as the overseer of humanity.

As a result, we have raged out of control spiritually in the churches. Different bible translations and biblical interpretations have led many to believe that we are entitled to everything that we ever desired and want simply because we came to the Lord to be saved.

Some would even have you to believe that God owe us for coming to Him?

Behind the meaningful relevance to the word want, we see the words desire; and the word will. I am intelligent enough to understand that Theologians are often appealing to our need of want? [Philippians 4:19]

But likewise I recognize that we as a generation of believers have gotten stuck at that particularlace of contextual destination, setting up the determination to rebell against the greater definitive reveal in the meaningful relevance underneath the word want!

I hear David saying in introspect to the accepted definition of the scripture;

I will not exercise the desire of my own determinate will against the will of the Lord for me; I will control myself and allow the will of the Lord to be in the forefront of my life. I will not only reverence the Lord's will for my life, but, I will also follow and obey the will of the Lord, even when it doesn't feel good, or when it has placed me into the midst of unpleasant circumstances. He knows what's best for me!

I hear David saying; **I'm going to stay with the Lord and trust in the Lord until I die!**

As people; even of the churches most times, we are found bucking against the will and the word of God when it doesn't suit our desire for the lifestyle and or the manner of living from day to day; God has required for those of us who love Him; that we walk according to His will, not our's.

I have had members of the clergy to vigorously debate with me concerning the required lifestyle that God wants for us to live as blood washed believers; they are determined that we can live as we please, and have whatever we want!

Many of them even feel that it is the devil working against us whenever we didn't get what we wanted from the Lord; inspite of the fact of being sinfully disobedient to the Lord!

You just may been allowed to have whatever you want while living secularly unsaved and out of the will of God?

How often though can you actually say that you enquired of the Lord before acquiring those things?

You; most likely, never considered the fact that the devil came along to spoil you by giving you multiples of things; only to cause you to go sour on the Lord whenever you truly surrender to Him?

Your conversation will for sure sound like the average Christians who confess that they had so much more money and stuff before they ever got saved!

They have gotten swallowed up in the idea of all of the stuff; suggesting that the stuff that they have acquired sends the message of just how blessed they are being able to have whatever they want without being denied.

In today's society, that manner of confession bespeaks of the acceptable unblemished score on their credit report. You could have become a master at acquiring stuff and yet be just as cursed as the devil who is instructing you to get all of the stuff! Be sure that you are not on your way to hell!

Ministries alike my own ministry are often shunned and disdained; simply because a name it and claim it theology doesn't actually agree with the word of God especially here in the 23rd number of the Psalms; so I never adhere to the teaching, neither do I teach it myself.

The Father in heaven cares about how we are living and the true quality of how it is that we are caring for others; more than He cares about the heaping pile of things that we might acquire, telling other people that He was responsible for giving us those things; when He clearly never ever had anything to do with the fact that we acquired so much stuff.

Sometimes we are getting things when we are supposed to be giving things away to others; with the price tags still attached to those things! So many people of the churches have become so selfish and competitive; that they are totally blinded and incapable of even thinking of anyone else beside themselves.

We need for God to be our shepherd and our leader so that He will keep us from becoming overwhelmed and totally taken of the natural things that we had been able to acquire here in the earth.

Lay not up for yourselves treasures upon earth, where moth and rust doth corrupt, and where thieves break through and steal: But lay up for yourselves treasures in heaven, where neither moth nor rust doth corrupt, and where thieves do not break through and steal: For where your treasure is, there will your heart be also.

[St. Matthew 6:19-21]

Verse ~ One

As it is, many people feel that they are actually better; more authentic human beings as a result of the things they are able to purchase as a result of an inheritance; or of an acquired college degree; they have a better paying job and are perhaps more finacially secured.

The only real true guarantee that we have for waking up in the morning on the very next day is God!

What we are able to do today doesn't say that we will always be able to do the very same things every day; as our health may fell us unexpectedly leaving us totally incapable to work and to provide the desired style of living that we might have become accustomed to live.

Life is too uncertain in the flesh here in the earth to set our affection on the things that we have acquired. People in general have tendency to be so proud of the things which they have gotten that others may not have been so privileged to acquire.

> If ye then be risen with Christ, seek those things which are above, where Christ sitteth on the right hand of God. Set you effections on things above, not on things on the earth.
> [Colossians 3:1-2]

See it like so;
1. The Lord is my leader, and I won't try to tell Him where to lead me!
2. The Lord is my provider; I will come to the table with a grateful heart to receive all that has been set before me!
3. The Lord is my instructor; I will never attempt to teach my instructor, or make an attempt to inform Him; He knows what's best for me!
4. The Lord is my protector; I will never step out in front of Him to fight my own battles without Him leading me!
5. I worship the Lord, and I serve Him; I will never seek to dethrone the Lord, nor make an attempt to share the worship that is only to be given to Him!

You get the picture! David said; I shall not! We find through the aid of the scripture, that he stood behind the declaration of his own words, in his own behavior and his life.

It is the desire of the Lord that we are available to Him, according as He has chosen us before the foundation of the world to be productive to the cause of the kingdom of God. [Ephesians 1];

We were made for the glory of God; what glory would it give to the Lord for him to bow down to mere humanity giving us the desires of our heart even though we

may never even acknowledge Him nor worship Him as God?

It is an enormous mistake in error to believe that you can call God to the carpet and demand that He sit down to listen to what you have to say!

I suggest that you politely de-elevate yourself from your own exaulted throne to humbly enquire of the Lord, by no means do we ever demand that the Lord hear us!

God does hear sinners repent; of their sinful ways, and acknowledge Him as Lord and Savior; and He always hear the prayers of the righteous; but the face of the Lord is against them that do evil! [Psalms 34:16]

It really doesn't matter what mere sinful people have to say negatively against God; it doesn't change who God really is!

David settled the issue first when he proclaimed that the Lord is! God; is who God is before we ever came along on the face of the earth.

We see the disdain for God whenever people lose members of their families in death; they somehow feel as if God should have asked them first if it might have been alright if He would visit their family circle to end the number of the allotted days of their loved one.

To no avail, many people are living with anger towards God because they lost a loved one!

They disregard the fact that everyone else on the face of the earth has lost loved ones also! Somehow certain people feel as if God needs to answer to them for having broken into their cycle of living, they had everything just the way that they wanted it? Things were okay........................

Even in the most devastating details of our lives, we have got to understand that God is in control. We work a plan but, God works a master plan!

He always knows what He's doing, and He does all things well. In those times that we aren't able to trace the hand of the Lord to the point that we understand what it is that the Lord is doing in our lives, we must learn to trust that He knows what He's doing and walk with Him.

You and I; will have to be broken for the master's use. God simply cannot use us with the mindset that we are so accustomed to. God knows how to soften us and to make us pliable, and flexible to be an instrument worthy of the master's use.

Verse Two

"Comentary on The 23rd Psalms"

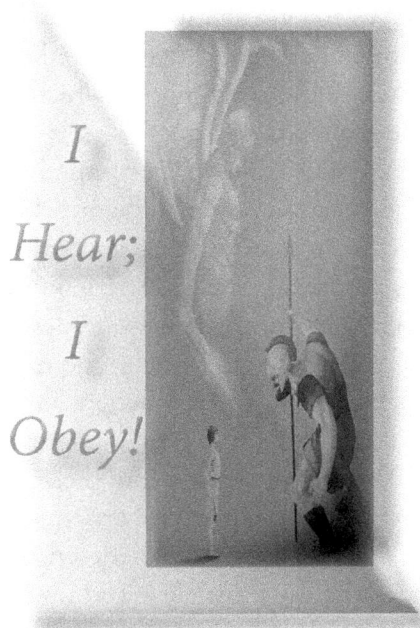

I Hear; I Obey!

He maketh me to lie down in green pastures: he leadeth me beside the still waters.
[Psalms 23:2]

"Two Formidable Words Which Express Directives"

Look again with me as we closely examine the cryptic details buried beneath the understanding of the words;"mak~eth" and "lead~eth."

I'm not sure why it is that we have misinterpreted the meaningful relevance of these two words. But it is very obvious that the true meaning has been diminished.

It is so misleading that the average person in the churches have been allowed to believe that God need only that we follow him when we have never been equipped to do so from the beginning. Many things that relate to us following the Lord as He leads us will require that we receive instructions to do so.

We used to have a service in the C.O.G.I.C church on Sunday evenings called Y.P.W.W;(Young People Willing Workers) as youngr people in the churches this is where they taught us how to behave ourselves as members of the body of Christ; even over and above that of the original Sunday School.

We were made better informed about what was required of us as children of the Lord. Just looking at other people in the churches could only give a slighted idea of what it

means to walk with the Lord; but how to actually take it upon ourselves to obediently move our feet while being led to do so, would require some teaching; in which we were often taught.

We will explore and comprehend the necessity for allowing Jesus Christ to Lord over us and to lead us continually to where He knows that our purpose and our destiny is truly ordained to be in the realm of humanity for the benefit of the Kingdom of God! [Romans 8:14; 28]

Whenever we look into these two words, the inexplicable consequence of failing to adhere to the engagement of the most clear and present admonition is realized as a result of shallow surface reading and the loss of indepth substantiated reasoning.

It's the suffix which levy the weightier attachment to finalize the definitive establishment in the more substantiated relevance enabling us to follow the meaningful dialogue, not just for comprehensive reading, but for applied obedience.

The base root words, make and lead; bear the weight of their own meaningful relevance; but, the added suffix to each of these words establishes the extended continuance and stamina to create an elongated flow in the definition, which supports the dialogue of the scripture suggesting to us to remain in the way of the provisional umbrella-like covering, allowing the Lord to do the very same for us even as He had done for the Psalmist.

THE SUFFIX ~ "ETH" AT THE END OF ANY WORD SIGNIFIES A CONTINUANCE, OR TO CONTINUE UN-INHIBITED; PERPETUAL CONTINUANCE WITHOUT FAILURE…….. (Author's definition)

David says; "HE MAKETH ME", for too long we have been allowed to think that God cracks the whip without giving us any type of a choice as to whether or not we are going to obey Him? But that is so far from the truth about God.

The issue here lies within the fact that we are not completely comprehensive to what the writer is saying about being made to lie down in green pastures.

The truth is that if we were already knowledgeable and capable of lying down in green pastures, we would not have to be made to do it.

Perhaps many would rather believe that it is the pastures that God makes for us; possibily suggesting for us that the green pastures don't already exist?

We are more familiar with sunburned patures; Amber in color and hue; but the greener pastures do already exist, and are made available for us to dwell there with the help of the Lord.

Unnecessarily, we are too embarrassed at the reality of not being

Verse ~ Two

familiar to livelier pastures of living, when all it is that we need to do is to relent and to release our emotions and let the Lord prepare us for better living, and better lifestyles.

What we know of is the fact that the possibilities are available, but how to go about living in the realities of such green pastures had not yet been revealed to us.

We want to be the persons already equipped to choose Green Pastures of living all on our own, but the truth is that we simply don't know, nor do we possess the skill to navigate our lives into such beneficial flourishing places of prosperity and growth in the natural and spiritual realms.

Make ~ to construct, manufacture, prepare, and or to formulate and to bring in to fruition. Even a better definition which might be more suitable for the topic of discussion is equip!

So; David is saying to us that; the Lord Equips him; having constructed him for being able to lay down in green pastures and for the ability to accept that those places are exact for the times and for the immediate need of our rest.

God causes us to be in places of upwards progressions of living when we should be sinking and daily diminishing, falling beyond our abilities to rise back up again.

It is the common practise of the readers to hurry past the beginning part of the statement; "He Maketh" and to get swiftly to the latter part; to lie down in green pastures; wich indeed sounds like the good part or at least the best part of the statement!

See it like so; He maketh; He puts me together excellently, and makes me capable for the task at hand, being fully prepared to stand in this place thoroughly finished and polished to represent God who set me here!

David says; "Me", in other words he is talking about himself and the benefits that has been awarded to him as result to being submissive to the leading of the Lord.

Often we can find ourselves focusing on others, commenting on the things that they seem to possess as blessings and the ora which surrounds them. We can always find it acceptable to applaud others for their prosperous demeanor.

We see that other people are living in the better built homes, that they drive the more high end automobiles; and the wear the top end name brand clothing! They are able to abide in places of financial upsurge which causes for then to be viewed more visibly acceptable to them that are seeking such personel of the community.

Perhaps David may be saying that I know that I don't deserve it, and

actually I shouldn't even be here; because I never had a clue as pertaining to what it even takes to be in such a place of living; but, The Lord has equipped me to be here, and He never let's me fail.

As life is always evolving, God puts his hands to my life to mold me again making me ready for the present circumstances which calls for me to emerge, being able to conform to the ever turning tides of my changing life.

The mindset of the religious communities at large is to repetitiously practice a religious regimen, though it does not have to be successive to any practical order of meetings or gatherings of any religious people.

Many; simply believe that every now and then we ought to acknowledge God and give Him the praise for everything that He has done; (*i.e. Thanksgiving; Christmas; Easter, etc…*) we should thank Him daily!

Even their mindset is often relative to keeping God first, they say; only, as long as He is considered to be number one on the list, it really doesn't matter about whatever else is in succession on the list?

The belief is that since God gave us our lives we should just go ahead and live to the fullest of our own hearts desires, no matter what it is that we desire to do, regretting nothing that we will have ever done.

Their idea of peaceful living is having no fear for God or man! Many believe that they should have a life free of all prohibitions. David's description of the Lord's leadership bespeak of God being in control of his life on a daily basis, but because He loves David; not because He cracks the whip like a slave master!

Many believe that they should go to church and hear bible stories; only they also believe that those stories are not necessarily for any regulatory practices for Christian behavior today, although they may acknowledge the bible as being true.

People of the religious society are detrimentally parallel to that of the secular humanist; human existence is exalted above and beyond the reality of God; whereas God is more of an idea to be explored and not necessarily the awesome experience of reality that He truly is; being God.

Having been in the church for all of my natural life, I have come to understand that so many people are unbelieving believers who go to church simply because someone taught them that church attendance was the right thing to do at least once a week (*on Sunday*), because there must be; or rather, there just might be a God somewhere?

Absorbed in the sea of their own questionable doubt of the truthful reality of God they have decided on church attendance anyway.

Verse ~ Two

They say that they believe that God is real and that His words are true; they just don't believe that God; being a God of love would ever be the same God to judge their behavior resulting in them going to hell for eternity; forever!

Somehow others are not so sure that God would divinely heal their bodies when we have physicians and medicine in the earth? People have been led to believe that God has lifted His hand from serving and caring to touch humanity many years ago?

As a matter of the fact; not many people really believe that God will forgive them for their hideous sinful behavior being that they have participated willfully having chosen to disobey on purpose?

People believe that their sins have erased or eradicated every possibility of God's delivering intervention to restore them back to the place of holiness and righteousness.

A lot of the very same people that believe that God is real, simultaneously they also refuse to believe that Satan is also real, and that Satan's kingdom reign is the real true enemy of the kingdom of God; thus creating the greater base for unbelief.

They seem to be stumped at the idea of once good angels of God; falling from heaven, now being demon spirits transformed to perpetuate evil in the earth's realm for as long as the earth remains?

They reject the fact that demons are the driving force behind their own wickedness and sinful, iniquitous behavior. As a result, they have ventured very deeply into the ideology which actually alleviates the greater awareness of good and evil?

So many preachers never even touch the issue of demons, or demon possession? But people with demon spirits on the inside controlling and destroying them spiritually are there in the churches in need of real true deliverance that can only come from the power of God in Christ Jesus!

We remember the story of the man who came to Jesus saying to Him;

> Sir, will you help my child? Foul spirits take him and they tear him and cast him into the fire, and throw him into the water; I came to your disciples but they could not cure him. Lord I believe; help my unbelief!
> (Mark 9: 24, John 9: 38)

Many people; for some reason or another, they fail to realize that God is concerned about the total man;

> Everything which concerneth me, God promises to perfect. [Psalms 138:8]

Since God knows just what is best for me; why would He not reveal those things to me knowing that I am in need of those things? What glory would it bring to Him?

I intend to show you how it is that God is not playing hide and seek with you, and neither does God

ever plan on leaving you to yourself to figure out the remedies for your sin riddled life.

The parenting scheme of many of the so-called parents of today may be to leave the children to themselves to develop their own ways of thinking and doing things in their lives, but don't get it twisted, that's not God's ways of doing things with His children.

It's common to hear people from all walks of life say; that, *"we are all God's children?"* However, through the scripture I hear the Lord contradicting that statement, as they are not all believing obedient children of the Lord through faith. All don't even believe in Him!

Most people can't understand how it is that God could still love them even though He has not been allowed to lead them? As a result, they just simply go ahead and assign themselves as being God's child, even though they are most disregarding of the scriptures and disobedient to God's word.

God does love us all; but He doesn't lead us all even in the churches because many simply refuse to surrender to His leadership and to His will. They don't want to hear Him; they want to be heard!

Question yourself and say; *"He Loves Me; but, Do I Allow Him Lead Me?"*

I can tell you assuredly that He desires to lead you as well as loving you! David says; "HE LEADETH ME!"

God knows whether we follow Him leading us or not! Amen! It is never enough to only follow God every now and then, niether just to follow Him from far off, if it is our desire to be declared as true followers of God.

If you are a church attendee, but also a practicing true rank sinner in every expression of your character on a daily basis, who never read or study the word of God and are consistently avoiding prayer, it is impossible for you to be declared as a follower of God.

Even if you do attend church and read the bible and pray, but you still find yourself going harder after the things of the flesh that only lead to sin and iniquity on a consistent basis, you are not a true follower of God.

Surrender your all to God and follow after the things of God and chase after righteousness hard daily and you will become a true follower!

It doesn't really matter that you may be sermonically lead astray through a message across the pulpit, if you never follow the leading of the Lord according to the written word of God whenever you leave the church anyway.

It's impossible to follow directions that you have never been given becuase the preacher failed to preach the truth of the word of God; or because you refuse to receive the word of God when it's preached; for truth.

Underneath David's statement I hear him saying; "He maketh me and He leadeth me, and I "alloweth," and I "followeth" Him." In other words, continuation is on both parts in the relationship with the Lord.

He continues to make me; to re-form me; He re-conforms me; to in-form me; and to establish me in His ways and I have no since of recoil with God as I allow Him to do with me as He pleases.

He guides me; He shows me the way; He enlightens my understanding and He fine tunes my vision to see what is ahead of me to prevent me from getting lost on the way; He keeps my feet from stumbling;

He catches me before I fall and He keeps me from hitting the ground; I don't take my eyes off of Him as He's leading me. If God can lead me, I can follow where He leads me!

But, his statement is not relative to following God at one time or another; it's about a continued obedience to follow the leading of the Lord daily.

Jesus teaches us in the scriptures to drop all to follow Him. [St. Matthew 16: 24]

All things of influence must be put aside and removed from the frontal lobes of our thinking capacities giving way to the process of thinking on the Lord and His word of truth as the driving force to influence the capacity to make and to follow decisions of righteousness and holiness to please the Lord in our daily walk of faith and Love.

"He Disciples Me***

Here, David is trying to get us to understand that the Lord is his master! Almost in parallel to that of the puppet master in the circus that is responsible for every move and action that is made by the puppet.

It is the plan of the Lord to love us into fulfilling our destiny and obeying His word; He loves us.

A first look focus of seeing a man lying down in a field of green grass is not the actual picture that David is actually trying to get us to see.

Any one of us could go and lay down in the park or out in an open field of green grass all at the behest of what we might ascribe to be the leading of the spirit of the Lord, but we would soon realize that our literal ability to do according to what we have read in this scripture would be totally wrong and out of contextual meaning to this written message.

We would soon want to also blame the spirit of the Lord for all of the insect bites or should a snake slither and roll up on us in the grass and any other attack or discomfort that might come as result of lying in

Psalms Twenty ~ Three

the grass.

MASTER - [NOUN] 1. A PERSON WITH THE ABILITY OR POWER TO USE, CONTROL, OR DISPOSE OF SOMETHING: A MASTER OF SIX LANGUAGES; TO BE MASTER OF ONE'S FATE. 2. AN OWNER OF A SLAVE...

Look at the obedient submission of David to the mastery of the Lord. Let's look at David's acknowledgement; he cared that the Lord saw his trangressions and that the Lord knew of all of his secret sins and indiscretions!

Even of the slightest unbalanced decisions that are made on a daily basis, God sees them and He knows all about them.

It doesn't make good since to try and continue on forward living as if whatever we've done never mattered, as if our sin doesn't stink in the nostrils of God!

David took the responsibility to ensure that he never developed a hard callused heart towards God as result of willful sinning, and self-indulgence.

> Have mercy on me, O God, according to thy loving kindness: according unto the multitude of thy tender mercies blot out my transgressions. Purge me with hyssop, and I shall be clean: wash me, and I shall be whiter than snow. Make me to hear joy and gladness; that the bones which thou hast broken might rejoice. Hide thy face from my sins, and blot out all my iniquities. Create in me a clean heart O God; and renew a right spirit within me.
> [Psalms 51: 1, 7-10]

It is extremely important that we acknowledge when we have sinned against God according to His word, and repent seeking His cleansing touch to purify our thought life to the point that He becomes the master of our thinking.

If we don't allow God to be the master of our thinking He can never be our Lord and our leader! It didn't take a rocket science for David to realize that he was standing in the way of his own deliverance.

It was already obvious that he was his own problem; so he turned to the Lord who is the only one that can fix it all for humanity!

Only He who is the *"Master;"* could create something on the inside of an alive; living breathing being already in existence, to make them new, all over again.

God is the maker and the creator of all mankind; i.e. "human beings," although David's request of the Lord here is of a spiritual nature and not at all physical, he recognizes that God is the all excellent spirit, everlasting and omnipotently subsistent to change all that is wrong with every human being.

He acknowledges that we are responsible for the things that we do in our bodies in the natural, but, it takes God to realign us to the place of spiritual cleanliness and righteousness.

Although we are often acting out

in our natural bodies, behaving sinfully and outrageous doing those things that are pleasant to appease our flesh, we know for sure that what we are doing is contrary to the mandate of the scripture; the driving force behind the actions that we have chosen is spiritual in essence, but carried out in our natural bodies.

We can't handle the spirit from the standpoint of any methodology of the flesh; it takes the spirit of the Lord to handle all of our spiritual needs.

It is the responsibility of every man to turn themselves over to the salvation of the Lord, surrendering our self-will to the will and to the word of the Lord.

Without a doubt, God is going to make us what He wants us to be, but we must surrender to the plan and to the active manipulation of the hand of the Lord moving in our lives.

Even though there may be times when the hand of the Lord makes us uncomfortable, and it may place us in unfamiliar territory. All of this will be okay if we only realize that it is the Lord making us as He will and desire.

Many things that have happened our lives have not been for the purpose of killing us literally, but it has been for the purpose of making us new from our heads to our toes which include our mind, body, and our spirits.

We have got to be made ready for the place where God will lead us else we won't be able to survive in that place, even though it may be that wonderful place of blessing!

Understand that God is making us for a divine purpose of intention and for a predetermined fulfillment of success.

Mirrors are made from glass; but not all glass have been condition to project the reflections of the things that pass by alike that of the glass which has been recondition and constructed for the purpose as to that of a mirror.

It takes God to make you to be what you truly ought to be, so as to reflect the true Character and Nature of God!

"To Lie Down In Green Pastures"

Understand that it's not only important to know what it is that God is making out of your life; it is equally as important to know where it is that you are actually being prepared to be located as the awesomely manipulated entity.

Where; is important to God; He will not just lead you to any unreceiving, unacceptible place incapable of receiving the ultimate skillful regenerated fashion of His own hands.

As Jesus taught the apostles;

should you end up there in the midst of unreceiving people, turn and shake the dust of the ground from your feet as a testimony against those people. [Matthew 10:14] [Mark 6:11] [Luke 9:5]

God is still at work in you, even since the time that you were first made, God is not through with you, and for some He has not even gotten started, because they refuse to be laid down.

From your birth until this point of your life, you have been in the maturation process of developing the understanding of who you are.

Some people have been caught up with trying to figure out who they are in the natural, which has hindered their ability to realize who they are in the spirit!

They can't know themselves, so ultimately they can't get a real grasp on knowing God. In confusion and fear they refuse to lay down.

Greatness in God requires a sweet surrender, that enables you to allow the Lord to make you to lay down. David assures that the place of humbling was indeed full of life and of growth itself.

Our struggle is because we want to know why the Lord would even want us to lay down?

In truth; most of us would give the surgeon trouble about having us to lay down during an operation; so they apply anesthetics to gain the control.

I can tell you for sure that everytime the Lord will lay you down is not for the purpose of getting something bad, evil, or ungodly out of you or because there is something wrong with you; rather it is for the purpose of putting something more on the inside of you, because there is something right with you! God; connects with God! God; knows where He is; and He knows where He is not!

Growing up in the C.O.G.I.C church; they used to sing a song which says; "My Whole Body Belong To God." From that time until now I have been blessed to get an understanding of what those older saints were talking about!

There is no way for the Lord to use our spirits without having the use of our bodies firstly. Many people in the churches are inflated over their thinking abilities, so they are determined that God will use them as result of their minds, but they struggle to bring their bodies along for the journey.

God will never leave us alone to go out on our own without His leading and His guidance. Many people are powerful thinkers, they know how to journey in their minds! Believe me, people have traveled to some far away places in their minds, if they were to tell you where they have gone mentally, we would be certain that many of them should be declared mentally incompetent, because their bodies never went on those journeys with them.

In case you didn't know, journeying requires that we pack up and take all of our being with us; every part of us! Reading expeditions are good, and being able to travel in our minds have proven to be beneficial at times; but God needs our whole body, soul, and our minds. [1 Thessaloninas 4:1]

Otherwise; we would be to the likes of a car without a transmission and a steering wheel. The motor in the car is alike the mind in our heads; it is very powerful and it has the power of control to push the automobile at very high rates of speed.

But, we never see a motor going down the highway or the street alone of itself carrying passengers; the motor must be accompanied with a body, chasis, a frame and definitely a transmssion!

Just as it is totaly impossible to see the mind of an indivdual waking down the street, or sitting on the couch watching a television show.

We see people walking down the street and wonder to ourselves; where is their mind centered and focused; what are they thinking about?

Without the legs of the body and the transmission of the car there is nowhere to go, because there is nothing to move us from where we are to the place of where we need to go; and definitely no way of following the directions to get there; you can't follow any path without the steering wheel; even though you may know exactly which turns to make and which curves are just ahead of you!

We should never step away from the leading of the Lord to follow after the ways of the world or of some other leading influence to go after that of which following the Lord would never lead us to it.

It pleased the Father for David to be an avid follower of the Lord; even as it pleased the Father in Heaven for Jesus to be obedient to the cross of Calvary; the grave; and the ressurection from the dead.

Obedience simply pleases God to the point of blessings and spiritual freedom and deliverance. (See; Abraham); [Genesis: chapters 12;-15;]

Obedience is the relenting give on the inside of us which refuses to please one's self; whereas its target is always to the outside influence of authority, power and leadership of rules, mandates, governments, and all behavioral stipulations of laws for regulatory practices of living among the society and the churches.

Of course in this case of study and recognition, our focus is God! Those who struggle simply to obey; they are often outright rebellious

and self-driven to please and to satisfy themselves, disregarding everything required for establishing them as obedient.

You will have to learn to trust God before you will ever be successful at allowing Him to lead you, and even before you learn obedience to the word and to the will of God.

Trusting God is a key elementary foundational platform to much of that which had been stated by David in this second verse of the 23rd Psalms.

Most people are not going to lay down anywhere for anybody that they do not trust, especially even God!

Something about the individual would have to bespeak of reliability and accountability before we would allow ourselves to be relieved from our own personal positions of authority and control.

As David tended unto the sheep out in the pasture in light of the sheep being attacked by a lion in one instance and a bear on another, as God strengthen him to rescue the sheep, he also learned that God could be relied upon at all cost and in the most extreme situations! David learned to trust God with his very life on the line!

I have met many pastors of churches who were satisfied to be declared as the congregation's leader, who were totally aware that the people were not following their leadership at all!

They were even determined to continue preaching sermons across the pulpit knowing that most of the people were not even paying attention to what they were saying for any purpose of adherence to their sermonic admonishment.

They could tell each member of the congregation personally who were not at all connected to their leadership, although they allowed those same persons a voice of influence in their ministries, of which often proved to be a serious mistake.

So many people have a negative voice of influence against the admonishment of the scripture, teaching that which is contrary to the bible and true holiness, but they are set on convincing others that they are true followers of Christ.

Jesus said; *"why do you call me Lord and do not the things which I say?"* [Luke 6: 46]

In other words, why haven't you learned to trust me, and to believe my words, and to obey them?

Why haven't you given your heart a chance to try me without reservation and hesitation? Even Jesus wants us to know what it is that motivates some to disobey Him yet their desire is to still call Him Lord?

It is forever impossible for the Lord to lead a rebellious disobedient distrusting people to a place of obedience where they refuse or simply omit to follow!

There is a place of ultimate blessings and esteem where mere men will marvel and desire to be in that place even as you have been awarded, where the Lord will lead them that obey Him.

There is a position of blessedness and glory to be envied, where the Lord desires to set us before the people of our surrounding atmosphere, but only the obedient followers of God will ever get there.

Following God means staying focused on God at all times being mindful of the fact that it is too easy to lose sight and focus; followers must always keep a fixed focus on the Lord!

Many people that have learned over the years only to look at God have never learned how to focus on the Lord?

Nowadays, many people definitely know how to surf the channels of cable and satellite television networks; in other words they have learned to look at channels as they pass on to the next channel; however they often fail to focus and to stay on the channel where they have stopped to view whatever is showing at the time.

Something of another previously scanned channel to the channel where they had finally stopped to view the programing of their choosing has gotten their attention simultaneously.

On a consistent basis, we are daily up running and moving around in a hurry uncontrollably seeking after that which is needed and often necessary for the welfare of our lives, too busy to even take the required hourly rest of sleep that we need to make it from one day to the next.

We have actually given too much power to the statement "self-preservation is number one!" This principle of living is often learned and practiced before we ever learn the principle of the word of God.

For reasons as of such, many people have never known the blessedness of lying down in the presence of the Lord!

For your heavenly father knoweth that ye have need of all these things. But seek ye first the kingdom of God and his righteousness; and all these things shall be added unto you. Take therefore no thought for the morrow: for the morrow shall take thought for the things of itself. Sufficient unto the day is the evil thereof.
[St. Matthew 6: 33]

It is to our own detriment that most of us learn to think about ourselves, having none to very little faith in the almighty God who is sufficient to supply all of our need, knowing what our need is even before we ask.

He knows what the supply will be, before our need even presents itself to us to be introduced to the Lord for our need to be fulfilled.

Psalms Twenty ~ Three

Too often those who say for a truth that they truly believe that God is able, they don't trust God or exercise faith in Him.

They are dragging about within themselves on a daily basis, dead ineffective faith; figuratively speaking! They have faith that can do nothing simply because they lack hope having no expectation of God!

GREEN- NAIVE AND LACKING EXPERIENCE, ESPECIALLY BECAUSE OF BEING NEW TO SOMETHING; YOUNG, NEW, RECENT, OR FRESH;

PASTURES- GRAZING; FEEDING PLACES; USUALLY FRESH GREEN FIELDS

The Lord fashions me and remakes and molds me to trust Him as I lay down my own will and my own ability to rely on my thinking and feelings so that He can teach me something new that I had never known before.

While He is preparing me to rest in uncharted territory, unhandled; unmanned;' unclaimed; undiscovered; uncontaminated; free from the painful past experiences of my life; I'm going to a place that has been newly prepared for my arrival; and it's a place that we can be sure that no one else has ever been made knowledgeable of, because it's a place prepared just for me!

God will break us down when he is preparing us to be used, as we will have already been molded and shaped by sin and iniquity, hard experiences and situations that ripped all of the strength and the truth from our innermost beings.

We find ourselves explaining to God the things that he already know about us, as an excuse for being truly unusable for the benefit of the body of Christ.

Many are led to believe that they may have a legitimate excuse for not having been delivered and prepared for the master's use. The only reason that any person would not be ready for the master's use would be that they had never surrendered to His will.

We; who are of the churches, only think that we are already ready to be used by God because we've been in church all of our lives, but God knows the residue that will have been attached to us as we innocently unintentionally make contact with the wrong people along the way.

Truth is that, there are a lot of ungodly; bad things that we can pick up on while in the local church with all of the ungodly and unsaved people who are in the churches fighting for a right to be equated as viable to those who have been blood washed and changed by the power of the Holy Ghost.

People's problems are often along the lines that they want to do what everyone else has done, just the same way that they did it! They have no desire for change; they prefer to do business as usual desiring to take the helm of leadership; behaving themselves just as the other leaders did who failed to please the Lord.

The infinitely wise God; He knows that we don't get change in the churches until He makes the changes! Doesn't matter how we may kick and fight trying to buck up against an imminent change, the fact is that a change has truly come for us. The greatest place for us to be in is in total agreement with God!

He Leadeth Me Beside the Still Waters:

As a young teenager I can remember hearing my late pastor say; "STILL WATER; RUNS DEEP!"

Then of course he would begin to expound upon the saying to us, although his explanations didn't reach the depths of my intellect until I'd matured as an adult, and had begun to preach and to teach the word of God as a minister myself, as the number of metaphors for the contextual meaning of water, are so many.

Being both metaphorical and realistic, the very depth of this saying can be rather elusive leaving those of us that hear the saying foiled and flubbed of the actual understanding, relatively based on the season of our lives, where we may be in the time of those seasons (at the beginning, in the middle, or coming out at the end); and of course our willingness to hear beyond the verbal resonance of the spoken words.

Whether it is the result of a learned behavior or of the natural propensities of certain individuals; we have the established patternistic associative photosynthetic ability to recall the movement in the water of streams and rivers, lakes, the ocean and even in the sea.

It is even common for us to see the water in motion as we turn on the faucets and as we see the water rising from the waterspouts of fountains; but what is still not the common occurrence for us, is to see the absolute stillness of motionless, non-rippling water!

The slightest, miniscule penetrating objects seem to always disturb the surface of the water causing the visible motion of rippling effects, of which is not only a common occurrence in a body of water, but also the natural response to the fluidity of most natural liquid elements.

There are many explanations for still water and even for the statement of saying "still water;" whereas in my own opinion, based upon what I have both seen and heard in my own life, some founded yet many unfounded explanations are given.

The ability for the water to stand

still motionless is dependent upon the containment of any particular aquatic body of the water itself, which will lend any truthful relevance to the actual proof and explanations for the stillness of the water.

Some often view the metaphorical examples of still water, as meaning peaceful and tranquil in light of respect as being motionless, where there are no activities or threats of flooding to overflow its boundaries; while yet others may see still water in depiction of life itself' of which I am most agreeable;

Everything on the face of the earth in one way or another is still associated with water, since from the beginning of the foundation of the earth!

Nothing that lives on the earth can exist without water refreshment to prevent the body from dehydrating and overheating. In the cognitive mindset of even the most basically natural recollection of water in our lives;

Water is often associatively interpretive to represent trouble or some type of a dissociative mentality of chaos and turmoil in all types of warring spiritual disasters.

For an instance: back in the year 2004, I dreamt of what appeared to be the ocean on what might have been a normal windy day under the cover of a very grayish clouded sky as if a terrible storm was brewing.

An emerging large army of foreign soldiers in complete military uniform, armed for war, began coming up out of the water marching upon the beach where I was positioned in the dream.

In this dream I knew that the water was productive of enemies to all American life and livelihood, possibly even also to the welfare of the church and or to the ultimate cause of Christ among the American population, as I had a school of the prophets on this same beach!

There are many ways to interpret the meaning for the dream, depending on the mentality and the spirituality of any individual.

The other elements in the dream bear the weight of significance to give relevance to the actual meaning, but the weightier matter of the dream to me was specifically the water, in that an army is marching coming up from the depths of the ocean as if to have been marching across the ocean floor, thus being able to reach American soil undetected?

A military mind might see this as an amphibious assault on America as a war zone for a vigorous battle for which we might be prepared for the war, but they were taken by much surprise!

In this particular dream I'm teaching the prophets in a class well attended with people who were

Verse ~ Two

seeking instruction to know the working prophetic order of those actually called to the office of the prophetic in the Kingdom of God!

For some reason we adjourned for a period of recess and were outside on the beach when I noticed the army arising up out of the water.

Just as Pharaoh and the armies of Egypt also ventured into the Red sea in pursuit of Moses and the Children of Israel; and were swallowed up in the depths of the same Red Sea as the water closed in upon them.

Metaphorically; the water was a depiction of trouble, but a greater hidden cause of trouble was actually arising out of much visible trouble that was already happening among us.

It was necessary to prepare the prophets of these times to be spiritually attuned to the coming turmoil and the assault against the body of Christ according to [ll Timothy 3:], the perilous times of which we are living was rapidly approaching, whereas the prophetic word for these times should show the people of the kingdom of God, directions to the peaceful tranquilities of the Lord in the midst of the chaos and war, both naturally and spiritually.

For reasons of such as these we who are of the bible believing and bible reading communities are often reflective of the miracle of the parting of the Red Sea so that the Children of Israel could cross over on dry land [Exodus 14:]; and even the crossing of the Jordon river may also come to mind. [ll Kings 2:8,14];

We need desperately to understand that there are times in our life that while we're symbolically in the midst of troubled waters, God would simply have us to be *still*!

There is going to be times when alike the Apostles who were in the ship out on the Sea of Galilee in a turbulent storm fearing for their lives literally; Jesus comes to the edge of the ship and looks out over the raging sea in the storm and says; "*Peace be still!*" [St. Matthew 8: 26]

All of the times we won't be blessed to be standing on the bank of the seashore to receive the word of instruction, as in the case of Moses; "*stand still and see the salvation of the Lord!*" [Exodus 14:13]

We understand being rescued from the tragic circumstances that arise from the water that may have overflowed its boundaries and flooded our living space; such as when flashfloods will have brought in much rain water, even more than was originally expected.

More than the earth's ground surface can hold sending the excessive amounts of water overflowing in all directions looking for a place to rest finding none but destruction in its path; and when hurricanes have

brought the water from the ocean and the seas inland.

There will be those times in our lives that we are symbolically struggling to prevent drowning in our sorrows and our troubles.

I know that we are geared towards taking survival measures to ensure that we don't drown and go under the tumultuous waves of trouble and doubt that come our way.

The detriment of most drowning individuals is that they are often flailing and splashing around in the water in a state of panic as if somehow to make the water behave; though in the moment, they are afraid of dying and even in fear of their lives!

But, if they could think to trust God because He can make the water behave and to just simply still themselves in the midst of that troubled situation, they might recover and eventually live emotionally, sociably, financially, spiritually and perpetually as a result of focusing on the outside of the situation where the provision of God is.

Yes in reality, we get swallowed up in the midst of the situation that we may often find ourselves in the midst of; but it's time to catch hold of the greater reality, which is God; knowing that nothing is more powerful than He is, and nothing has the power to take you under as long as God is on board with us.

See, there are times when we finally mature to understand that God is always around and with us, that we also realize that we could never be in any serious trouble knowing that we have peace with God!

Wherever we are, so is God; He never leaves us alone in any situation, especially those situations that may be too much for us to handle.

BESIDE - ALONGSIDE, BY, NEAR, NEARBY, NEXT TO, ADJACENT TO, CONTIGUOUS WITH;

The clarifying definition bringing to us the present understanding here is beautiful in that it helps us to see the provision of the Lord.

David never said that He leadeth me into the still waters; *he said that He leads me beside the still waters.*

Still Water; can very assuredly be referenced to the fact to mean that it remains to be whatever it is! It is still water; period! It doesn't become something other than what it is now that God who is the creator; is on the scene.

What we are often saying about our all omnipotent God; unintentionally we are erroneously placing Him on the same playing field as the witch-doctor; soothsayer; warlock; wizard; and the workers of dark spirits of the underworld?

Because we don't do a better job of research and biblical study with prayer and fasting as a manner of those who are acquainted with the

Lord; we often suggest without knowing that God will perform some type of hocus-pocus, or some type of a mysterious magic to get things done for us!

If God has to change things from being what they are in an effort to move in our midst, it would bespeak of the possibility that He may not be as powerful as we have been told that He indeed is? [Hebrews 11:6]

The very reason that we need God to initially lead us is for the sake of knowing just who God is!

Whatever our situations may be, God can handle them just as they are to us in the same time that we come to Him to fix things for us. God; is God!

David; at the very time of writing this number of the Psalm; he was in trouble running and fighting for his own life. This is the reason that he never took the occasion to kill Saul who was indeed in pursuit of the life of David.

The situation was just as it was when David first began to flee for his life! God was there in the unstable situation with David whereas he never had to lean to his own understanding and take matters into his own hands.

David didn't wait to call upon the Lord only after he knew that Saul had died and was dead in his dust; but he called on the Lord when Saul was in hot pursuit of him.

You see even in the midst of your trouble, your situation has not created a troubled zone or an atmosphere too foggy and obscure for the Lord to lead you through it and out of it into the next dimension of your life.

David was just about to become the king that he had been anointed to be; therefore the kingdom of Israel had to remain as it were, else David had been fleeing actually for no reason at all; even to reap that which had never been promised to him; had Israel been totally transformed?

Perhaps so many people have not been delivered of that; they have not had their situations changed, because they are often looking for God to fix *that*; when in actuality they are in the midst of *this*!

They are looking for God to begin to work over there, when the trouble that they are in is right over here; or finally they are expecting for God to fix it later on, when in fact tey are in trouble right now!

David is running; but in actuality he is not necessarily running away from Saul as much as he is running into the previously anointed destiny as the King!

He was running into his destination, although he had to run through certain situations and through some things to get to where God had ordained for him to be.

God has to lead us because often times what we see on the sur-

face is not even the actual cause of the trouble that we're having most times.

It's not at all on the surface; you have got to be willing to go beneath the surface to get to the bottom of the issues that you have, in an effort to find the viable solutions that are the conduits which allow the peace of God to flow through the situations to rest upon your total being.

On many occasions people are looking for the cause to the problems that they are having, but when they don't see the cause at the surface of their search, they give up on seeking to know the cause.

No wonder, more people are not living in peace and following the Lord on a daily basis; they are chasing after that which has not even been revealed to them. They're running around in circles having no idea where they will land as result of their own aimless mission.

Many people make the mistake of jumping into a pool of water not knowing the true depths of the water; they are willfully jumping in to the situations unprepared with very low expectations as to how to get out of what they had just gotten into. The deeper the water is, it will actually take a bit more time to resurface, and it will call for more breath in the lungs of an individual to make it back up to the top.

As a skilled swimmer I am aware that there is a difference from even being plunged into the depths of the water, and intentionally taking a dive having a preconceived knowledge of the true depth at the bottom of the pool.

At each scenario; the individual will have been submerged a little deeper having been plunged into the water much less prepared than would be to that of the skilled diver who also have the skill to calculate the depth of the dive.

A very popular colloquialism among the people of today is the saying; "It is what it is!"

It's still water; it's still trouble of all sorts, for all reasons, with and among all people; But, God; is still God!

"Comentary on The 23rd Psalms"

Verse Three

I'm Restored To Follow!

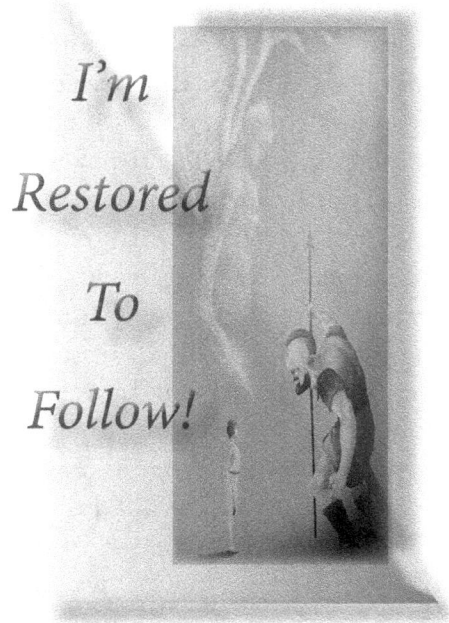

He restoreth my soul: He leadeth me in the paths of righteous for His name's sake.
[Psalms 23:3]

Defragmented; Put Back Together!

As we walk this walk of faith and love in the Lord, we suffer many diverse attacks that are designed to rip us apart, to destroy us. Many things that rattle our cages dividing our piece from our peace; every part of us is rumbled and shaken!

No need in thinking that we can just get happy on our way once we have been born-again without the help and the leading of the Lord.

There are many obstacles and hazards intentionally thrust into the middle of the way as we sojourn through time on our way to eternal life; we will definitely require the Lord's guidance and His help.

When we know anything, we are discombobulated, and confused, bewildered and mentally scattered. Our present circumstances are allowed to separate our destiny from our purpose, changing the given direction of our intended destination. Living has got a way of causing us to end up in a place where we were never prepared to be!

Life's happenstances, have such impacting effects on our mental configurations so that we may

be found upside down where we used to be rightside up.

These are the times that we are found allowing verbalizations to flow from our lips that are so far from our character and spiritual demeanor, that should never be heard coming out of us!

As it is my friend, the enemy wants us to take it back! He wants us to agree with him in saying that it was all for nothing; we could have been better off going in the opposite direction away from our callings and away from the Lord who called us.

People are hurting so deeply, they often wonder what it is about them that God would allow them to be so cut and bruised that nothing seems to heal them where they are hurting the most? Seems as if almost no one really cares about the pains that they feel.

The claws of the enemy have left them tattered and ripped into pieces so finely that it feels as if no thread could ever stitch them back to gether, and for certain no glue could successfully bind then back together in one piece ever again.

Alike the valley of drybones in Ezekiel 37; they're asking; Lord can these dry bones live again?

I know what it feels like to be too hurt to pray! Have you ever been so hurt that the words won't come out of your mouth? You know what you intend to say to the Lord but the words just will not cooperate with your lips as you attempt to form the words to come out of your mouth.

These are the times that we may find ourselves serving the Lord, but without gladness! We will come before the Lord with singing, but never songs of praise and of worship; we come singing the blues and moaning trying to release the pains!

For a truth real things happened which caused us to be in need of help and healing; we need to be made whole. The very people that we have trusted to love us and to care for us, they have left gaping holes and wounds in our heart and our spirits.

Contextually misplaced, is the mindset to think that we can emulate Abraham's methodology of journey to please the Lord; when in fact the Lord had never called us to do what He did call Abraham to do!

One thing's for sure of this life of salvation in Christ Jesus; we cannot live this life of spiritual transformation and behavioral change on our own!

God wants what He asks from

us as result of our call; everything that we may choose to do is not acceptable to God.

It is often most difficult to get people to understand that God has got a way already established, for enabling us to live successfully as faith-filled spirit-filled citizens of the Kingdom of God; in the midst of doubters and hateful unbelievers.

Living godly requires preperation and knowledge for the journey of righteousness. It is disasterous to plan on going nowhere! But, to have no knowledge of getting there in the first place is degenerate!

We can be seriously deceived to embrace the idea that God will release us to this world's system to chart our own pathway of faith and believing. The word of God is our road map and manual of instruction for a faith building lifestyle that is pleasing to the Lord.

David's relationship with the Father in heaven; meant setting his feet to a pathway uncharted by his own will that he was not traveling on before he came into the covenant with the Lord!

God's; own established pathway of righteousness is clear and of total assurance; having the strong binding adhesiveness of the accuracy of His word; tightly held together unmovable, definite to enable us to reach our intended destination to complete the personalized predetermined assignment given to us before the foundation of the world. [Ephesians 1:4-5]

So many people make the mistake of statrting off on God's ordained journey for their lives but with their own ideas of how they are going to reach their destination, without any biblical imput and not very much prayer? The ideas of fasting putting themselves away for a time of setting themselves before the presence Lord is out of the question.

This is often the reason that so many people of the Christian faith have determined to go out on their own to live and to mix with the rest of the world, as if everything had already been done for them; not needing any of their participation?

Not so; but we do have a more awarding method of handling the reoccurring situations that plague our lives on a daily basis through the indwelling power of the Holy Ghost; which will keep us safe.

The answers and the solutions to the questions and the problems that we are sure to face in this walk with God are already established and installed into the

written word of God. We really are too blessed to be stressed!

In the churches; so many people are looking for a life that doesn't really live; a living that isn't accurately alive in the true and physically tangible world of actuality in reality!

Jesus; taught us through the written word of God that;

in this life we shall have tribulation and offenses, period! [St. John 16:33] (empheses added)

Regardless of what the outcomes are going to be as result of the offenses and the tribulations that will show up in our lives, whether positive as a result of having Jesus in our lives, or negative for those by whom the offenses and tribulations are initiated, the fact is that tribulation and offenses are going to happen in our lives!

Erroneous disconnected religious theology alienated from the true spirit of God, and the lack of inner-spiritual comprehension to the word of God; have got people looking for churches that are totally error free and already holy.

My friend; be it known unto you from now on that that kind of a church just doesn't exist here in our natural realm of living.

Having seen so much of the world's influence among the people who confess to know God in the power of His love, others have given up on the idea altogether of a church that mirrors the very image and spirit of the Lord?

Nevertheless; far too many people are yet on a never ending quest to find what they are looking for in an organized church, rather than to just find God in Christ Jesus; in the fullness of His power through the indwelling power of the Holy Ghost.

This reality of being restored is consequencial simply because people have wandered off into the wrong direction, and they are totally off the track; alike trains, seriusly derailed!

As we look again into the life and times of David; we are thankful and worshipful to our God for allowing such an awesome and obedient servant of the Lord to be an example to us even of these latter ages and periods of faith in the Lord.

People; in general, are so determined to sensationalize the lives of the people listed in the Holy Written King James Bible; placing them on a much higher plane of living, as if they were some sort of alienated super spiritual human beings; much different than to that of us who live in this now present generation of people?

They were all people like as are we, however many of them might have been a bit more dedicated and committed to their relationship with the Lord.

Our purpose for seeking and searching the written dialogue of the scripture here in the 23rd number of the Psalms is so that you, and I as well could be even greater examples of faith in righteousness and holiness to others, as David has been to us.

Today's seekers; many of them at best, they are spiritually obstinant; subconscious wonderers and nomads of faith; tossed and driven by the winds of every available doctrinal system of belief available flowing through the streets of any community in the society.

They are not just double minded alone, they are polygonal and extremely perplexed in their thinking capacities, whereas they alone have no idea as to whether any of their acquired ideology can produce a direction desirable for the benefit of an intended destination to reach God.

Having no since of direction to find the true pathway to God, being obsolete of trust for any biblical knowledge, they have no exact affirmative faith replica to profound the benefited resolve of their search!

Which eradicates the possibilities for any firm platforms on which to allow their faith to rest assured and unsinkable!

Their likeness of faith is therefore destitute of buoyancy to sustain up-righted faithful statuses against the raging religious and scientific tidal waves of angry stobborn and rebellious resistance to their acquisition of faith of God in Christ Jesus.

Although, as result of their stagnant unexercised faith, they are often looking to sources outside of their knowledge of God in Christ Jesus for answers to their questions, and looking to the world to make since of living with all of the painful occurrences and circumstances that happen to plague their lives.

Not a whole lot wrong with being able to look around your own space of living and atmospheric bounds of knowledge available to you to find answers; until only, you have decided to erase God out of the equations, having determined that you no longer need Him.

We; who have matured in the faith of God, we know that God has all of the answers written in the word of God; however, we must prayerfully walk with God

in faith and stay in the teaching atmospheres where the word of God is being taught and exaulted above all that of which we have been taught in the secular society, outside of our faith in God!

faith cometh by hearing and hearing by the word of God. [Romans 10:17]

Having predestined us according to His own purposed plan, He only knows when His perfect plan has been accomplished in our lives!

I endeavor is to get the people of faith in God to look into the written word of the bible first before going into any of the secular areas of knowledge in search for the answers which only hinders any believer from being able to clearly hear and to discern the unmistakable voice of God.

If only you would learn to trust in God, you would soon discover that there are times that God will speak through the means of the other natural resources only to get a clearer message over to you, but He doesn't speak through everything!

As David lived surrendered to God; again this wording is suggestive of the continued uninterrupted hand of the Lord on the life of the shepherd boy.

We realized in verse Two; the suffix "eth" has been added to the descriptive words of the attributes of God's shepherding leadership.

We again see the continuum of God's mercy and grace over the life of David as he describes for us how God kept His unchanging hand on the purpose and the person of David.

God never changes His mind concerning His will and divine destiny for our lives; God never changes His love for us, as He is love.

My heart is saddened as I reflect on the massive number of people who have fallen away from the Lord in total rejection to living saved and sanctified to again live a life riddled with sin and iniquity, haven chosen to ignore the shameful guilty weight of sin.

They have allowed themselves to successfully silence the sensitivity to regret having ever committed any acts of sin, refusing to believe that they have never done anything that would make a difference in the relationship to which they have developed with the Lord through faith and repentance.

It has become common place for many people in the churches to ignore warnings of devastating possibilities as result of sin and iniquity once they have reattached themselves to the very momentous ride of forbidden pleasures.

On any given Sunday; one might just hear a sermon suggesting that it is God; Himself; who have set these forbidden pleasures of sin immediately in the way of the people of the churches as a means for testing their true allegiance?

I have never read anywhere in God's word where He could ever have anything to do with sin or iniquity other than to cast it away from His presence to destroy it in hell!

Knowing the deceitfulness of sin and of Satan; God would never trust leaving humanity to handle sin on our own! Satan lives in the midst of sin; though most often undetected!

People are so busy feeling good in the midst of sin, they can't sense that Satan is also there, because they also refuse to accept and to acknowledge that Satan lives in the midst of all sin!

No matter how we might have been intellectually manipulated to think about certain acts of sinful living; the very sacrifice of Jesus Christ on the cross of Calvary is still in effect the most prevalent truth and strength of the gospel of salvation that forever erradicates, and annihilates all sin!

Through my own research and study in the word of God; I have found that the scripture has been taught erroneously with selfish intentions;

A feel good theology to provide a preventative cushion against the need for a personal change of lifestyle, not needing to develop a true behavioral testimony reflective with the intent to confirm that we had truly been washed in the blood of Jesus, and cleansed from our own sinful guilt and responsibility; has been taught instead.

I find that too many leading the churches are willing to argue over what is truly the sinful practices of the people of the world according to the written word of God and what sin they feel that God will actually excuse mankind from the guilt of committing as a lifestyle choice!

Just as you and I have got a reason for turning to the Lord for salvation in the first place; God's got a reason and an eternal plan for saving you and me!

We can't do whatever we want to do and still get into heaven with the Father! The living choices and the lifestyles of people on this earth will forever keep us out heaven and send us to hell instead!

"Restoration of the Soul"

Considering the necessary process of restoring the soul of man; it is imperative that we first understand that as a result of willfully engaging ourselves into the behavior of sin bodily, mentally and even spiritually, knowing that sin, iniquity, and all transgressions were forbidden, the residual telling evidence attaches itself to our souls with the intent of never letting go!

We actually become the downward spiraling slaves of wickedness as result of allowing ourselves to be used to fulfill the satanic scheme of transgressing the laws of God; whether we did so with a rebellious attitude or had been led deceptively into the darkened schemes of self and Satan.

As a boy; even as a young adult; I enjoyed playing any number of outdoor games with my family and friends.

After being outside for a while, we were in need of a bath, as our body's fragrance was good for outdoors and hardly noticed, but, the moment that we decided that we were coming in, it was obvious to everyone that had been on the inside that we had been outside playing, exerting our energy and sweating. We stank!

We may have left the balls and bicycles, the animals and our friends also, outside; but the residue of the games and the aroma from the outdoor atmosphere came inside with us! Quite a noticeable difference in the fragrance of indoors and the scent of the outdoors. Whew!!......................

And so it is in the realm of the spirit; those who stay on the inside with the presence of the Lord growing and increasing in the fragrance of the spirit of the Lord, they can smell you whenever you come in out of the world of sin, living as you please, according to your own will and desire; unbeknownst to you; you reek of the enemy!

Too often there is a stench among the sweet smell of the people of God, revealing that someone had stepped away from the word and the will of God, only again to test the ways of the world and sin, compromising the beautiful fragrance of God; the sweet fragrance of holiness; having submersed themselves into the disappointing rebellious disgusting odor of Satan. Satan stinks of everything that is against God!

For we are unto God a sweet savour of Christ, in them that are saved, and in them that perished : to the one we are the savour of death unto death; and to the other the savour of life unto life. And who is sufficient for these things? For we are not as many, which corrupt the word of God: but as of sincerity. But as of God, in the sight of God speak we in Christ.

[II Corinthians 2: 15-17]

I doubt seriously if anyone had to tell David that naturally he smelled of the wild whenever he came in out of the fields, after tending to his father's sheep?

It's the nature of the flesh to to give off a scent whenever the body has exerted energy to the point that we have begun to sweat, and we also pick up the scent of the environment we've been in and of the people or the animals that we've been in close proximity to.

Many people won't come in out of the world simply because they don't want to clean up; they say that they are not ready to change and to give up on the ways of the world; they have just gotten comfortable with the stench of their sin, and Satan.

The residual attachments are like so for example;..............

Many predators of the oceans and the seas have parasites and other small aquatic members that annoyingly attach themselves to the other larger fish but without permission, leeching off of their blood supply, and living off of the scrap food lost during a kill as to ensure that nothing is wasted of the meal.

Many of the predators and larger fish also bear what may often appear to be very painful scars and open wounds from haven been cut against the rocks.

Though many of the scars could also be the result of predatory attacks upon their bodies likewise to that of the prey that escaped their attacks; truth is that they do scar themselves against the rocks desperately seeking to get rid of freeloaders.

Marine biologist have closely scrutinized the bodies of many aquatic mammals and the likes of all that would be considered to be predators or large aquatic feeders, observing the parasites and leech feeders attach to their bodies, only to realize there was nothing that they themselves could actually do to free them from the discomfort of the freeloaders.

Just as the larger mammals of the sea cannot free themselves of the parasites and the other freeloaders without scarring themselves badly against the jagged rocks along the coral reefs and the sharper edges of the rocks closer to the shoreline; we our-

selves cannot free ourselves of the residue attached to our souls without the shed blood of the scarred and broken body of Jesus Christ on the cross of Calvary.

Once sin and iniquity have been allowed to attach to our souls, the required scarring bruising and slashing of the flesh and even death is required. The blessing of Jesus Christ the savior and redeemer has resolved the issue; we need only to adhere to the sacrificial work of Christ on the cross of Calvary.

He is despised and rejected of men; a man of sorrows acquainted with grief: and we hid as if it were our faces from him, there is no beauty that we should desire him. Surely he hath borne our griefs, and carried our sorrows: yet we did esteem him stricken smitten of God, and afflicted. But he was wounded for our transgressions; he was bruised for our iniquities: the chastisement of our peace was upon him; and with his stripes we are healed. Yet it pleased the Lord to bruise Him; he hath put him to grief: when thou shall make his soul an offering for sin, he shall see his seed, he shall prolong his days, and the pleasure of the Lord shall prosper in his hand.

[Isaiah 53: 3-5, 10]

This is the reason figuratively; that so many people of the earth are bleeding and wounded, sinfully bleeding the guilt of their own wickedness all over everyone else that they come into contact with!

It is simply because they have spent so much time attempting to do for them, that which only God could do and has already done for us through the sacrifice of the only begotten son of God!

Thank God for Jesus Christ; He did it all just for you and me! Your wounds can heal; your bruises can now be diminished and vanished away; He was chastised in our place, and we know that we deserved to be chastised for our own foul behavior; the stripes that He took on His own back assures that healing will be manifested in our own sick bodies; through the blood of Jesus Christ!

I am of the opinion that the reason so many people are trying to discredit Christ Jesus; another deity allows for one to disconnect from the responsibility of the guilt and the shame of living foul and ungodly according to the written word of God in the holy bible.

Thus also alleviating the need for individuals to seek having their souls restored, fixed and scrubbed clean through the powerful blood of Jesus and the word of God.

But at best, the efforts of man are all null and void! One can be encouraged to ignore the responsibility of the soul, however, no one can disregard the day of reckoning in the judgment of the soul!

We often wonder how it is that these wounded mammals of the deep are able to go on forward swimming through the ocean and the seas with jagged rips and tares in their flesh as if to suggest to us that nothing ever happened?

Likewise our souls get wounded battered and torn, but, God is there with a remedy for the pains that we bear giving us the strength to go on forward as if to suggest that nothing ever happened to us either.

When the cares of this life succeed to get us down, whereas we are down on the ground; thank God for His mercy, which is there to lift us from the ruins of our fall;

It is of the Lord's mercy that we are not consumed; because His compassions fail not. They are new every morning: great is thy faithfulness. [Lamentation 3:23]

Many times the pains that we suffer are the result of the behavior of our own choices. Foul behavior causes us to lose sight of the fact that God sees all things at all times, whereas whenever we come running back to Him, were it not for His mercy, He might often turn us away from being restored.

Most people would leave a bleeding skunk wherever it's found, laying there to die, or dead and stinking! Sin and iniquity, and its open wounds, stink like a dead skunk; the mercy of God allows Him to reach past the total disgust of our true status and the causes, to free us.

Doctors of theology; psychology; sociology and psychiatry examine mankind daily observing that people are spiritually and emotionally tied in a knot weighted down, but often beyond any assistance of their expert knowledge and skill.

They are often unable to free them from the binds and the heaviness of their guilt, even though they have offered solutions and have suggested behavioral changes to them.

Guilt and condemnation are uninvited freeloaders; whereas many people develop ways to try to deny the guilt of sin and to silence the pains of condemnation; they soon realize that there is but one way to totally free the soul; accept Jesus Christ as Lord and Savior!

The salt of the ocean and the sea is powerful enough to heal the wounds in just a short time as long as the fish continue to swim in the salty water without the scent of the blood of their open wounds inviting other predators to finish killing them.

In other words, God already had a plan set in place, to aid the fish of the ocean and the sea to heal, and to deliver the post-wounded parasitic bodies of the aquatic dwellers which had been sliced against the rocks and ripped by the sharp teeth in the jaws of the other predators of the deep, as they escaped death.

Likewise, there is healing for the sin sick and wounded souls of all mankind on the face of the earth. We need only to adhere to the established plan of salvation and deliverance and dwell there in the presence of God!

Being restored is necessary because the open wounds of the soul are invitations to greater wickedness of sins and iniquity, they become entryways for demon spirits and for a resting place for Satan who should never find rest in any of our souls!

We cannot afford to distance ourselves from the presence of the Lord knowing that we have very weighty dark residue attached to our souls, pulling us down to the pit of hell, beyond the bottom of our graves!

The average salt water fish never intentionally swim out of the water to stay for extended periods of time without the threat of imminent death; though there may be a few exceptions.

The soul is in no way comparable to that of old cars, furniture, sailboats, train locomotives or anything of the such that the thought of restoration is giving high priority. Our aging soul is the most precious possession that we had ever been given, we cannot restore our own soul!

Most people are knowledgeable that all mankind have a soul, but the true definition of what the soul is and its purpose actually has not yet been realized within their scope of reasonable thinking.

Most likely, this is the reason, that far too many people of secular influences and lifestyles are willing to sell their souls or give it away to the highest bidder for the biggest pay-check?

The soul; *(soulish realm)* is the seat of the emotions in every man. It may be better understood when thought of as the control board of the feelings and emotions of all people (alike the control board of a PA system);

Verse ~ Three

Some people are so darkened and dull in their feelings and emotionless whereas they appear to never feel anything or to be emotionally stirred by any occurrence, no matter what; there is little doubt that they ever had a soul; but they do have a soul!

They are just in need of having their soul saved and delivered from the power of sin and death, through faith and repentance; which will reactivate their ability to feel and to respond accordingly to what they are feeling when necessary.

David; said; *"he restoreth my soul;"* I sense that David is speaking in reference to a continued process of tweeking the sensibility of the soul whenever in need of being restored.

RESTORE- IS THE PROCESS OF PUTTING A PERSON, PLACE OR A THING BACK INTO ITS ORIGINAL STATE AND PLACING IT BACK TO ITS ORIGINAL POSITIONAL.

So, therefore we see restoration as putting a thing back together in its original state and then setting it back upon its original place of rest.

Too many teachers of the scripture have the people of the churches and Christian Organizations, so-called; believing in religious systems of Christian behavior that suggests that God wants us to be good, and that being His only real desire for us as human beings?

That is, my fellow kingdom dwellers; the greatest deception and the most washed out and the more weakened presentation of the truth which will allow any one of us to do a very good job at making hell our final destination!

Consider the fact that before Adam and Eve sinned in the Garden of Eden; before they knew good and evil as result of eating the forbidden fruit of the tree; they knew God! They really knew God!

Knowing God; overshadowed the need to know anything about being good, or doing good, or having anything good about themselves in anyway!

We are sure to acknowledge the fact that the people of the world have evolved and changed since that day back in the garden; I will also acknowledge that the sinful event which took place in the garden is the reason that the people have evolved in character and spirit that is so far away from that of God!

Adam and Eve; were more like God than any sin could ever teach them to doubt or to inferiorly embrace as now being a sinfully lessened creation of

nature, as a human being.

It is my own opinion; that in the original, initial state of the human formation from the dust of the earth that the soul in which God breathed the breath of life, the soul itself knew that it was in a godly place within us until sin was allowed to enter!

All; For The Purpose of His Name*

To those of us who really do care to practice and to observe integrity, we go out of our way to protect our names.

It is important that our names are not be-smudged and disdained, causing disgust to others as they hear the very mention of our names; as a result of our own past behavior.

Too often we have been led to feel that protecting our names is of the utter-most importance in and around the body of Christ.

The last time that I checked the scripture, relative to the most important name, in the book of the Acts of the Apostles; we are informed;

there is no other name given unto men whereby we must saved other than the name of Jesus! [Acts 4:12]

Of the most familiar and heroine impacting story of David; where he faced the giant Goliath on the battlefield, we are reminded of the power of David's defense, which was the Name of the Lord of Host!

It wasn't his sling or the five smooth stones that he put into the script and the slingshot, these were only successful as result of the trust that he had in the Name of the Lord of Host!

From the end of the earth will I cry unto thee, when my heart is overwhelmed: lead me to the rock that is higher than I. For thou hast been a shelter for me, and a strong tower from the enemy.
[Psalms 61:2-3]

The name of the Lord is a strong tower: the righteous runneth into it, and is safe.
[Proverbs 18:10]

And an highway shall be there, and a way, and it shall be called the way of holiness; the unclean shall not pass over it; but it shall be for those: the wayfaring men, though fools, shall err therein.
[Isaiah 35:8]

Jesus saith unto him, I am the way, the truth, and the life: no man cometh unto the Father but by me.
[St. John 14:8]

The precious name of the Lord justifies and establishes the sociable standard in the privaledge of holiness and righteousness in all the earth, among men of any community; to all who call on the name of the Lord!

Mere men of sinful influence

and determinate self-will, err and falter greatly in the establishment of their own righteousness, simply because the awarded advantage of the name of the Lord is attributed to those who not only believe, but have received and have confessed the name of the Lord; (*"Jesus Christ"*) without a doubt!

Unbelievers; the ungodly and doubters are not awarded the same benefit of the name of the Lord; as result of their faithless-ness and unbelief.

They miss the truth of reasoning, which is that the things that the Lord will do for any of us that believe on His name by faith, is even more-so for the benefit of the great name of the Lord; rather than for any bragging rights, as result of the blessings!

So many people arrogantly allow themselves to believe that they are more special than the average person, or even perhaps more favorable to the Lord than others; they believe that what the Lord is doing for them is far beyond the scope of the average individual's thinking capacity and their ability to be as special as they are themselves; being able to receive by faith?

I take much pleasure in bursting your bubbles; God has declared that He'll do it all for you, but for the sake of His own great name! The blessing indeed is yours, but the real benefit belongs to God!

The resonance of the name of the Lord in all of the earth and the spirit realm is as the fallout of the radiance of a Nuclear Mega-ton Bomb!

Everything in the pathway of the bomb's fallout are either transformed; totally destroyed; or at the very most disintegrated leaving only the dust of the ashes of what was once an object of some sort.

The power of His name; will do what no other power or authority can ever do.

David said; *"He leadeth me in the path of righteousness for His names sake….."*

David could've possibly gone astray to the left or maybe even to the right, as any man on the face of the earth can do at any time of their lives, especially should they become too inquisitive or bored with their present circumstances.

But I believe that he recognized that it was indeed the Lord leading him straight and forward in the path of righteousness; but what is key is the fact that he comprehended also that it was for the purpose of

the Lord's great name!

We have no ability on our own to successfully complete the task of the Lord and to please the Lord without the covering protection and ingrained compass of the spirit on the inside leading us in the right direction, to the right people and in the proper timing.

God; in His infinite wisdom, He knows at all times the things that we have never even considered, for the simple reason that those things have never even entered our ability to mentally fathom the possibility of those things even being a true reality;

The things that God is going to manifest as a reality in our lives, will be at His own discretion and purpose of timing.

Should the Lord leave us to ourselves to make our own ways in this life, not only would we all end up in a ditch eventually, but we would also exhaust all of our own allotted time and space upon the face of the earth, while meandering around lost without hope. We'd quickly come to the end of our own ability, even sooner than we could ever imagine!

We're limited whereas God have no limits; from everlasting to everlasting, God is! He always was; always is; and will always be!

The infinite supply of God's resources places Him far beyond any created human being in all the created realm of the cosmos.

It was gravely important for David to bring us to the understanding that God will do some things for us so remarkable that we would be overwhelmed and forever impressed at the idea of having been the recipient of such graceful deeds of kindness and love, beyond that of even our earthly parents and loved ones. [Psalms 118:23]

Yet; as I repeat myself, he also let it be known that God's reasoning for doing such wonderful things for us would be for the sake of his own great name!

God gave His only begotten son for our salvation because He loves us so; but He personally puts His own hands to guiding us and leading us to and through His own command for our righteousness.

The awesome thought of God leading us to ensure that we get it right and that we find and reach our destiny is just as great as God is Himself!

The great and mighty deeds of God's presence and love are proof to humanity that He is as great as the great representation of His matchless name.

Goliath defied the name of the Lord our God in the presence of all the armies of Israel and Judah; being a Philistine rebel to the image and to the very holiness of God by his own deviant nature, he was aware of the truth and the reality of David's God!

The Philistines knew the power in the resonance of even the slightest mention of the name of the Lord of Host. It struck fear in the hearts of the rebel armies and the enemies of the tribes of the Israelites. [1 Samuel:]

Remember: Pharaoh of Egypt; acknowledged that Moses' God; is God! As God put forth the terrible plagues against the Egyptians, they were forced to realize and to acknowledge that God is the only living God!

Elijah; down at the river Jabbok on the bank against 450 of the prophets who sat at the table of Jezebel, and 450 of the prophets of Baal;

Through the awesomely manifested act of fire falling down from Heaven on the water saturated altar of Elijah, where the fire licked up all of the water on and all around the altar, while simultaneously consuming the animal sacrifice and all of the wood to make the fire and the altar itself; those evil prophets were brought to the opinion that God; is God!

Although it cost them their lives for haven been opposed to the truth of the God of Abraham; and Elijah at that time; they had to admit based on their own witness, that Elijah was correct.

So it is to this very day; so many are in need of convincing of the Lord's true reality. People have heard of God but they have not yet been acquainted with Him personally.

They have been told that God will do some things for us that no one else could ever do; but they are of the opinion that God will only do those thing for the sake of pity, which is totally erroneous and could never be further from the truth.

The truth is that God doesn't depend on any of us to totally validate His name; while as a true worshipper of God it is our place and purpose to cover the name of Christ through worship and praise.

God will act according to His own name whenever we trust and ask in His name through faith.

We as people are often intrigued as we look over the

Psalms Twenty ~ Three

vastness of the land and the sea, and even of the whole idea of the earth and the sky.

The name of the Lord blankets it all simultaneously, being in every space, at all times!

We can never be everywhere at all times, seeing to the needs of all humanity and the beast of the fields; the fish of the sea; the foul that fly through the air; and of course of all the inhabitants of the earth?

Creeping things that slither and slide on the ground and that live under the ground; insects and all of the life forms that fill the space of the earth in spaces too small for humanity;

But to our own amazement, God is there, everywhere supplying life to plants and to animals alike.

As science seek to provide the answers as to the reason that all things exist, and how it is that they are able to thrive and to grow producing after each its own kind, the true answers lie with the very name of the Lord!

[Genesis 1]; tells us of the fact that in the beginning God created the heavens and the earth; and all that there is in the earth to this very day!

Because so many choose to be doubtful of the truth in the word of God;

God; who moves by His own spirit; He does so for the benefit of His name, to establish the truth and the eternal reality of His presence in the earth, even in the presence of the doubtful and the unbelieving.

It is important that all believers come to the understanding that God doesn't lead us and guide us just because; or because He's the great bully in the sky, but for His great names sake will He do all that He will ever do for us!

We all have come into contact with people who claim to be personally acquainted with the Lord God; who have absolutely no actual proof other than a bible in their hands.

But to those who allow the working of the spirit of the Lord in their lives through the power of the Holy Ghost; there is undeniable evidence through the moving hand of the Lord that they are indeed in relationship with God!

Whenever we confess the Lord, God; He will validate the relationship to those who have heard and believed our testimony of true salvation and relationship with the Lord.

Even though the Apostle Paul; through his own confession, he acknowledge that whenever he

Verse ~ Three

would do good that evil was present with him! [Romans 7:21]

I neglect not to inform you that even as I was a sinner and I did some sinful things; as a blood washed believer in God; there have been those times that whenever I would have considered doing wrong, that God was present with me!

Preventing me from doing those things that I would have done that would testify in negativity that I had ever known the Lord! [Romans 8:] Remember that all have sinned, which includes me too!

God leads the righteous through temptations and through the stressful desires of sinning as a mere human being. God; awesomely keeps those who truly want to be kept of the Lord, from doing the things of satanic influence and unrighteousness; outright!

Through weakened excuses, so many people of the churches worldwide continue to make the attempts to pollute the name of the Lord through their own wicked and sinful behavior; though many are not always aware of the fact that the sin that they are comitting is trying to distort the name of the Lord through their actions.

But no need to worry, God is standing by for the sake of His own name to wondrously provide proper conduct of humanity and the spiritual behavior as an effective witness for all who call on the name of the Lord and truthfully desire to live right among their families and people of their surrounds!

Nevertheless the foundation of God standeth sure, having this seal, the Lord knoweth them that are His. And, let everyone that nameth the name of Christ depart from iniquity.

[II Timothy 2:19]

God is forever calling for humanity to come out of sin and iniquity as a way of living on a daily basis, but as we are incapable of coming out of sin on our own, He is there to help us.

Even though God has given us a mandate for living righteously, it is never the plan of God for us to accomplish righteousness on our own ability.

That which is often presented to us for righteousness can often be self-righteousness, or simply put the righteousness of the flesh which is against the will of God for our lives.

The righteousness of mankind is at best an afterthought to that of which God has intended for all mankind in the earth. Through the washing and regeneration of the blood

of Christ through the word of God; righteousness for all mankind has been established.

Through faith and repentence, the blood of Jesus have signed our names, therefore God knows who we are by our names;

Knowing that we need him to do it for us in that we might become more closely acquainted with the power of His name; also having the ability to successfully share the name of Christ to those who might believe on the name of the Lord.

David said at first that the Lord restores him; so after putting him back to a place of godliness and cleanliness, it is also necessary for God to lead Him to further places of righteousness and peace in the Lord; our God.

God will bring you out of sin and unrighteousness, so long as He is allowed to lead you to the greater places and the pathways of righteousness and peace in the Holy Ghost.

Thank God that we have David's example to this kind of relationship with God our savior and our redeemer; we need only to emulate the structural balance for which David was able to maintain a communicable relationship with the Lord.

Nowadays, many people of the churches desire to practice the powerful presence of God, but they are in even greater need of having their behavior altered to reflect the righteous relationship that they have been awarded as result of truly being washed in the blood of Jesus Christ!

But it is all for His great name sake!

Verse Four

"Comentary on The 23rd Psalms"

I Walk; With God! No Fear; I'm Safe!

Yea though I walk through the valley of the shadow of death, I will fear no evil: for thou Art with me; thy rod and thy staff they comfort me.   [Psalms 23:4]

The Comfort and Security of the Keeper

Now unto him that is able to keep you from falling, and to present you faultless before the presence of his glory with exceeding joy, to the only wise God our Savior, be glory and majesty, dominion and power, both now and ever. Amen'.   [Jude: vs. 24-25]

WALK ~ 1. {INTRANSITIVE VERB} - TO MOVE OR TRAVEL ON LEGS AND FEET, ALTERNATELY PUTTING ONE FOOT A COMFORTABLE DISTANCE IN FRONT OF, OR SOMETIMES BEHIND, THE OTHER, AND USUALLY PROCEEDING AT A MODERATE PACE. WHEN WALKING, AS OPPOSED TO RUNNING, ONE OF THE FEET IS ALWAYS IN CONTACT WITH THE GROUND, THE ONE BEING PUT DOWN AS OR BEFORE THE OTHER IS LIFTED. 8. TO DISAPPEAR OR BE STOLEN {to steal away; author's definition} 11. TO BE RELEASED FROM PRISON OR FOUND INNOCENT OF A CRIME.

{NOUN} – 1. A JOURNEY MADE ON FOOT, ESPECIALLY FOR PLEASURE OR EXERCISE. 2. THE DISTANCE TRAVELED OR THE TIME IT TAKES TO GO SOMEWHERE ON FOOT. *Encarter Dictionary; USA*

This topic of discussion is not only relative to having a hands on effect of our relationship

with the Lord; it is more-so relative to having our feet applied and unmovably fastened to our own charted paths of life, even when those pathways are leading the way to what might be uncomfortable situations for us.

It is most necessary that we walk through our valleys whether they are the valleys of death, or simply our own valley experiences where we are at our lowest periods of living.

Walking through these times of our lives assures that we are able to see, apt to learn, analitically aware to glean from our surroundings, and that we are a cognitive witness to how the Lord helped us and how He brought us through to bring us out of our valleys.

The detriment of so many people is that they are in a hurry to come out of their situations; they either want to run through their valley situations, enabling themselves to avoid seeing the things necessary for them to come out on the other end of the trial better than they were before they entered into it!

Others spend time wishing and desiring that they could some how or another take wings and fly away enabling them to totally avoid the trial all together; disregarding everything about the experience, period!

They don't care to see it or to feel it or even to know about it! They have convinced themselves that such experiences are totally unnecessary, or point less to them; even though they are in the midst of all types of valley situations almost daily!

The only thing that you need to get in a hurry for is to slow down and to take your time to be sure that daily you walk with God, and even through your valley.

Anything that we enter into without the Lord being with us, we are not awarded the assurance that God is going to be with us whenever we come out of it! That being said; take the Lord along with you in every trial,; every battle; every valley and of course into every wilderness experience.

If God is in the midst of the valley with you, you need to know and to be assured that He is not there just going through the motion disconnected from the personal effect that your valley situation is having on you, but He is there navigating the way for you to go through it all to come out on the other end victoriously!

Oh; if only you could understand how much the Lord delights in walking with you; it is so pleasing to the Lord to have you assure Him that you are pleased to be with Him even in your own valley experiences! As awesome as The Lord is; He knows how much we want Him in our affairs.

There is a difference in wanting the Lord to fix things for us so that our lives are running smoothly; and wanting the Lord with us because we Love Him, and believe Him!

God knows all of our selfish motives and the intentions of our hearts. He's aware that most people only want the benefits of being aquainted with Him; and that they are not at all interested in knowing Him personally.

I'm convinced that this mindset and attitude is the result of faulty erroneous teaching in the churches or the lack thereof? It's an assault on the spiritual well being of the people of the kingdom of God!

Those of us who have chosen to believe God by faith in truthful relevance to the point in fact that we have actually surrendered our will and agree to walk with Him in relationship and the fellowship of the word and the spirit of Christ, hoping in the eternal presence of His glory; we are blessed with biblical revelatory understanding and the faithful assurance of knowing that God is always watching over us, whereas; it is never a concern that we have wandered out of the God's sight.

God is everywhere (omnipresent) at all times and nothing and no one can evade the all-seeing eyes of God; God sees us in whatever state we are in wherever we may be on the face of the planet, even He's (all omniscient) totally aware of the thoughts that we entertain relative to our safety and our wellbeing.

God knows whenever we fear and are afraid; and He's aware of what it is that has actually chased us into the realm of being overwhelmingly concerned relative to the dangers of the unknown.

Never forget the fact that God also sees the wicked ungodly demonic behavioral patterns in how it is that they operate, being aware of the whereabouts of both Satan; and the wicked ungodly people of the earth; at all times.

So many are deceptively led to believe that Satan is some type of an entity that poses a real problematic threat for God?

It is not at all an issue of Satan vs God; people its God; period!

Satan is only able to influence those in the earth's realm who through fear and doubt allow him to do so in their own lives.

Satan is a formless evil spiritual being, an eternal spirit locked away on death row doing time in the earth's realm for which he was never created nor formed to exist! Satan has been forced to exist here in time without a formed body!

He had been created to live in Heaven with God until iniquity was found in him. [Ezekiel 28...] Therefore he has neither the natural form nor the spiritual subsistence to even be a formidable enemy of the Lord Jesus Christ; at best he's our enemy influence here in the earth.

Even the angels in heaven are greater in power and might as it relates to the devil.

Although it is unnecessary for us to fear and to worry having this knowledge of God, feeling that our backs are exposed to the enemies in our surroundings, there are times when the fear of harm and of insecurity may have a gripping effect on our mentalities as we endeavor to live and to provide a sense of welfare and security for our families, both naturally and spiritually.

Whenever we fail to keep a watch on ourselves, we find that we may have somehow allowed ourselves to wander into the realm of uncertainty!

It's normal for mere men of carnal thinking to evade the presence of God, refusing to ask the Lord to cover and to keep them, protecting them from all hurt harm and danger. Arrogantly they feel that they can do this all on their own natural abilities and education.

Only, too many people fail to realize that there is no natural way to physically fight the devil and evil spiritual occurrences.

Some way or another, people have decided against the security of the Lord, seeing that they have chosen lifestyles that are totally disrespectful and transgressive to the laws of God's written mandates in the word of God.

It is a very sick way of thinking; when hearing people say that they would rather suffer the consequences of their own choices of living rather than to be ruled and governed by God and the bible and seeing them adamantly carry out those lifestyles that assure their own eternal damnation!

People; who cannot even prevent or stop their appointment with death as every one living will have to face on the earth; they have been duped into believing that they have the ability to safely tuck themselves away from all hurt harm and danger!

Purported animal lovers; go all of the way out having close encounters with dangerous animals and brute beast of the jungles in the wild and in the depths of the sea. Too frequently, the price paid for the value of such chosen encounters is their lives!

They test closing the distances with themselves and the venomous bites of arachnids, snakes, bees, and all other stinging insects and animals; whereas whenever they are actually bitten or stung they get right back up from the deadly encounters, if and when they are blessed to remain alive, they get right back to meddling with the dangerous affairs of those deadly kind.

I have come to realize that truth is both parallel in the natural as well as in the spiritual realm; we are indigent to provide what is to be known and respected as totally secured environments of living in our natural habitats; in our spiritual environments only prayer is going to be the security blanket to ward off the offending spiritual enemies that seek to destroy our souls.

David was chosen to watchfully attend unto the sheep out in the pasture in the wild, for the reason of creating a safely secured environment for the sheep.

Someway, somehow; a lion and a bear, and only God knows what other predators; infiltrated the security of the sheep's enclosed gathering under the watchful eyes of the shepherd.

Seeing dangers alone of itself does not have the power to eradicate the eminent destruction as result of the proposed threat.

The places that we have believed to be secured and totally protected are infiltrated by enemies who threaten our livelihood, and sometimes they are able to cause lots of damage before they are discovered and captured, or neutralized from their ability to cause us eminent harm.

Going about our daily affairs, it is necessary to be on security alerts by our nation's armed forces who watch the borders of our country to prevent us from being overtaken by enemies to our welfare and our peaceful living; day by day!

Many of our enemies are already here on the inside living among us in our neighborhoods, visiting our churches, frequent-

ing our shopping malls, banking in our financial institutions and freely roaming our streets.

We cannot see or know of all of our enemies in the natural as we go about our daily affairs for reason of the fact that they are skilled at mixing and fitting in among the general populous to the point of un-detection!

They are not going to be recognized as a dangerous enemy of the people that they walk among at first sight. Preparation and skills are required for the purpose of detecting the secrtet spies who are hidden right in the midst of us.

So I am left to wonder just whatever it could be to cause people to become so adamantly distrusting of the Lord; thinking that if they deny the reality of the spirit realm then they can actually render it null and void to the point that it doesn't exist?

Jesus went to the cross to enable us to walk out of sinful lifestyles; never was He intending to excuse us while we continue to live as we please and continue on in sin being connected to the devil's agenda against the will of God through our lifestyles and our behavior.

New comers to the fellowship of the churches are better encouraged to take their time to make up in their own minds as to when and as to whether or not they are actually going to come all of the way over to thinking and doing things the way that the bible has instructed for us as believers to do them.

On top of the lies to influence people to come and to join their churches and to coax the people to be financially supportive, they begin teaching them that they are now eternally secured in God through their confessions?

Having only spoken a few words out of their own mouths, even though many may not have even successfully repented in their hearts, and for certain they have never forgiven the people of their past who might have harmed them in any way!

At best they have been allowed to become locked away on the inside of themselves refusing to entertain the ideas of biblical change or even to be changed.

Many may know of God; based on what they might have heard from a neighbor or a co-worker on the job, or had been taught in a Sunday school class, or maybe they heard about God in a prepared sermon during Sunday morning service, but they have not allowed God to know them intimately by His spirit; they

Verse ~ Four

have never met the Lord. [St. John 4:24]

They have actually no fellowship of the spirit, nor have they entered into a relationship with God the Father through the saving grace of the son; Jesus Christ.

So often misspoken and misinterpreted, this terminology, (*Eternal Security*); has left the bulk of the churches populous in disarray.

The situation is that people, most of them anyway, are seeking a one shot measure, whereas; they would automatically be secured and safely tucked away from the flaming penalty of hell; just in case hell really does exist?

Firstly; and foremost, most people in their own ways have made attempts at trying to erase the truth about hell out of the meaningful dialogue in the scripture. [Psalms 9:17]

Satan; has been further declared as only having been an alternative mythological figment of any religious mind, chosen as a means of excusing one for having failed to live according to the bible's mandates for mankind. (*"The devil made me do it!"*)

The mention of the devil on the other hand, has often been used as a tool to frighten some rebellious unbelievers into believing in the bible, many skeptical doubters say anyway?

Disregarding what the bible has spoken to us in the scripture, mere men have still chosen to close their eyes to the need to walk circumspectly in obedience to the scripture and to behave themselves differently from the ways of the world.

For this reason alone people have come forward out of the closet into the openness of public opinion to declare that it is now unnecessary for people to be governed by the Holy Bible.

People greatly desire much more, to go with what they are feeling without penalty or judgment of any kind, rather than to follow the word of God.

I might have to agree that people no longer care to be governed by the bible! [II Timothy 3:]

However in blatant disagreement to the findings of secular society, although carefully stating; I would say since the 90's here in the U.S.; it is not really clear anymore as to why people even attend the churches still?

People no longer have a determination to present Jesus in the manner of their own chosen lifestyles whereas others living on the outside of salvation can see the shining light of Christ; the hope of glory alive in their

lives and make the decision to come on over on the Lord's side to change their way of living.

The behavior from religious church people who are actively living out-loud in rebellion to the scripture have dangerously suggested to sinners that their consistent sinful manner of living may be taken into consideration as a newly discovered order of reality for people to live by; instead of obeying the teachings of the bible in the churches.

Since long ago; even before these present times, the secular societies of this world's influence have been in favor of the dismissal of the scripture, if it were possible.

The power of the word of God though, has always since before now put extreme pressure on every act of sinning and the satanic reign of the devil among the people of the earth!

People in the churches, don't mind sinning at all! [Hebrews 10:26]

The un-churched people of the society no longer see a difference between them and the professing believer on many occasions now?

People now see a diminished power of the local churches to dictate mandated behavior for all people.

We sort of get the feeling that even the Atheist have relaxed a bit to prevent the influence of the churches, as a result of the outright presentation of the now sin borne lifestyles of the leadership and the laymen alike in the churches.

It is dangerous when the people of society no longer see the church as any type of a threat to demand changing their godless lifestyle and behavior. [Hebrews 10:31]

But, don't get it twisted; this reality is to be lived day by day! There are no check-outs and off-ramps for pleasurable recreational time breaks to escape the reality of living godly to participate in the pleasures of sin for a season; if you go off, or get out, there is no guarantee that you will ever make it back!

Only, too many are willing to compromise their security in Christ Jesus choosing to mesh the practice of sinful indulgence with that of the life of salvation in righteousness with God; in Christ Jesus. [Hebrews 10:2b]

Alike the process of trying to combine grease and water; sin and salvation will never mix!

The one will cancel out the other when truly present in the lifestyle of any individual; it doesn't matter how adamant you are in telling others to please be patient with you because God is not through with you.

You may be the only one that hasn't realized that God has not been able to even get started with you; because of you!

One cannot be in salvation today and on the flip side, totally in sin on tomorrow! One lifestyle must be chosen over the other!

Mere men assign this type of mentality as to that of being liberal in their thinking process, when in fact my friend this type of thinking is dangerous and deadly both to the life in the spiritual and to the natural existence of all mankind.

The scripture has already declared to us that "the wages of sin is death!" [Romans 6:23];

However, people of all walks of life teeter dangerously on the edges of doubt distrusting that God could mean exactly what He has said concerning sin having death as the ultimate penalty.

Where would David have been found had he been out of the will of God; whereas he could not even hear the voice of God instructing him how to perform that which was needed in the time of being confronted with the lion and the bear?

We never know which direction the confrontation, or the storms of our lives are coming from always? So it behooves us to be on watch faithfully obeying the word of God so as to be attuned to the voice of the spirit when we need Him most.

Truth is; God is here for all of us on the face of this planet, but in the times of need many that have never been faithful to the Lord, they cannot hear Him; nor receive His instruction showing them the way out of their dilemmas!

They don't even know where to begin to follow the Lord or to believe in His power to heal or to deliver them from trouble or danger; as they have often chosen to avoid Him at all cost.

No wonder people are afraid and fearful at even the slightest hint of danger; ant mounds are like mountains to them! A cut or a scratch seems to reek of the possibilities of death; they are totally shaken to the very core of their beings.

This; my friend is not the valley of death that the Psalmist is speaking in reference to in the scripture, although sin is the ultimate cause for death in all the created realm of the earth. (*"The wages of sin is death"*)

Had there been no sin in the

Psalms Twenty ~ Three

beginning there certainly would not have been the reality of death! [Genesis chapter 3]

There is to be certain sense of fear had in the heart of every man in respect to the awareness of the eminent dangers of disobeying God in our daily lifestyles according to that which the scripture allows for us in the earth! Again the only problem is that many refuse to fear God in respect of His word.

We all have been made aware [Genesis 3:] how that because of disobedience and total disregard for the spoken commandment, the doorway of death was forever opened for humanity to die as result of God's judgment against sin.

Even though people are witnesses to the committal of bodily remains to the graves in the cemetery; somehow still the imminent reign of the terror of death seem to emotionally evade the general understanding that death has been tucked away just out of our sight on the inside of the pleasures of sin!

Sin's pleasures have the ability to blind people of the imminent penalty for the sin that is presently being indulged; as long as it feels good and it feels right for the present moment, don't stop.

In this dispensation of grace, most people don't just drop dead right in the midst of the sin they are committing, so somehow they think they just might have been cleaver enough to have escaped God's judgment for their sin, or they believe that they have been excused for committing sin simply because they are human-being?

For generations now, people; have bought into idea that human-ness means utter weakness, and excuseable frailties of the flesh; whereas the nature of sin is more powerful than the transforming reality in the blood of Jesus Christ; which enables us to resist sin in our natural bodies.

People simply believe that we can't help it; we have to sin because it's natural, so just let it be!

The fact is that whereas you the individual sinner have not yet been judged; as the scripture says; sin has already been judged and rendered unacceptable in all the righteous realm of God forever and doomed to hell!

"it is appointed unto man once to die, and after the death come the judgment." [Hebrews 9:27]

paraphrasing by the author;

So it is therefore obsolete and totally insignificant to continue to make the argument that no man can judge you; in the end

Verse ~ Four

it would have been far better for you if only man had the responsibility of judging you! God will judge you!

Except that we are washed in the blood of Jesus, sin; in and of itself is the working order of death in all humanity; death will have ocassion with every man on the face of the earth; no one is exempt!

Death is irreversible; everyone will die with the exception to those who are yet here to see the eminent return of Jesus Christ to rapture the church, at which point in fact the human bodies will be changed from mortal(natural) to immortality(spiritual); glory to God!

You may have already begun to ask the questions, why would the author write so poignantly about death and the wages of sin thereof; well I'm glad that you have asked!

David opens the dialogue of this particular verse, stating; *"yea though I walk through the valley of the shadow of death, I will fear no evil"*;

The man after God's own heart is speaking about the subject of death, for real!

Yet even so as he is a surrendered servant of the Lord; who, haven acknowledged that he recognizes that the Lord is his keeper; it had been made aware to him also that even the eminent curse of death is rendered powerless against him, as a witness to the fact, since his own enemies always failed to kill him, though they were trying sometimes daily, in hunt for his life. [1 Samuel 18:10-11;]

His message here remains available, clearly for the benefit of those of us who are the servants of the Lord; who having given our lives in sacrifice to the will of the Lord, many of us have discovered that we have enemies that desire to take us out.

Some say that they have no enemies? Sure about that? You are either uninformed or simply ignorant!

Those enemies show up in many diverse forms that may not always be in human form; to the likes of illnesses; diseases; physical attacks; accidents; weather disasters; wild beast and so on.........

Perhaps you have not come to the point in-fact of knowing what your enemies look like, or you are living in a fantasy land where you believe that everybody is just totally in love with you and all of your frailties, flaws, your inconsistencies, and of all of your mistakes.

Believe it or not, all of the neg-

ative things about us effect more than just ourselves, which have the tendency to aggravate others concerning us.

We know that one day we will die we just don't care to talk about it! We know that this life won't last forever but it is not one of our better topics of discussion!

According to the scripture, we know that Jesus Christ is coming back soon for the church, but apparently that doesn't appear to be a popular favorite topic for discussions either!

Yet We Walk

As we see people from all walks of life die daily, the very images and the realistic pictures of death are witnessed and realized!

Whereas; the very topic discussion of death and of dying may sicken us and with great fear sometimes may shake us to the very core of our innermost being;

We are all going that way as soon as God get ready for us and some will precede God's timing for their demise!

We walk through the valley and the shadows of death often as living on the earth will have it no other way.

Just to think of the many people who are living with terminal illnesses, and lying up in hospital beds, or even bed-ridden in their own homes or nursing care facilities; these people are actually in the valleys of death.

Satan is on death row, doing time until God says that it is his time to be put to death; [Revelation 20:10]

Every time that we come into contact with sin and Satan, we are on the battle fields against humanity, confronted with the same strategies of war to separate us from God; we are again exposed to the true causes of human eradication and death!

Exercising humanistic traits of sinful behavior is openly the manifested evidence of the presence of sin and of Satan in the lives of those people that commit the acts of sinning willfully in their bodies.

Not to mention those who are living on death row waiting for their own day of execution? On their journey, these people are made aware of the fact that unless the Lord intervenes they are scheduled an appointment with death itself!

Death has become more of a living reality for them more so than it is for the average individual, even though it shouldn't be; because, they are faced with

Verse ~ Four

documentation of deaths actual day and the time of arrival!

David said; "*Yea though I walk*"....

It is to our benefit to understand the contextual meaning of the word walk used at this particular inference in the scripture.

My definition; chosen for that sake of greater understanding to the Psalmist message is; "To STEAL AWAY!" David can be understood to be saying; as I steal away to be in exclusion to my self alone; it is not so because I am afraid of dying myself, but, rather it is because I need to deal with the dying of those that I love alone with the Lord.

Death is a low but a lonely place of existence; one can be swallowed up in greif should they be too focused on death alone, and not necessarily the ones who might have died?

But firstly; it is even moreso paramount to undertstand what he meant when he said; "YEA THOUGH;" most often this statement has been taken to mean even though I walk?

However; YEA is another form of saying YES! It is a statement intentionally spoken to the onlookers who see us as we go through our valley times but in their presence.

Others will often criticize and compare their comfortable times to your discomfort, with the intentions of causing you to feel inadequate and inferior to them in all of their display of pride and of arrogance.

So David looks at them and he says; YES; this is where I am at this time of my life; I'm taking my time to ensure that I come out of this valley; because whenever I do come out it will be over. The Lord is with me; I coming out alright; no matter of what it may look like to you!

Metaphorically and figuratively speaking; David refers to his walk as of a certain time period of happenstances, whether they were ordained of God, or just simply allowed.

There was the allotted period whereas David was either fleeing for his own life, or mourning the death of one of his own children, or his friends.

I get the feeling that David developed the determination of living whereas he says within himself;

"Even though I am face to face with these untimely periods of being challenged with death;

His enemies are constantly seeking to kill him; the sword is in his own house among his children, and people that he has known all along among his ser-

vants and his friends are dying all around him; still he says;

I've got a grip on living and staying alive as the Lord allows!"

David mourned the death of the Prophet Samuel; and of Saul and his son Johnathan; these deaths brought great sorrow to his heart.

Death exposed a much greater sense of human-ness in the life of David, even as it does for most all of us; yet he said in his own heart;

"I WILL FEAR NO EVIL"...

In this particular season of maturity as result of experiences and in wake of the fact that one have spiritually matured in the faith of Jesus Christ; it is a reality most assured to rebuke the fear of death and of dying.

We spiritually mature to the point in fact of approaching death at a funeral from a more confident aspect of reasoning, whereas we are not on the ground uncontrollably sobbing and weeping as if all of the hope of our own world has collapsed and shattered abruptly ending without warning!

We learn to control ourselves in the presence of the Lord knowing that death is not the end! As we are yet breathing and alive, we know that God's got us all!

Death is not the end of life; while it is the end of living in the natural body here on the face of the earth; it's the only way to physically exit living in time, and to spiritually enter eternity with God; the Father in Heaven!

It's impossible to exit life! Else there could be no life after death has ended the reign of naturally living on the face of the earth eternally in heaven with God; or in hell in eternal damnation!

Even if the seed which is responsible to produce after our own kind, is destroyed; the blood of which preceeds the seed is still there! Life is in the blood.... [Leviticus 17:11]

I now understand why it is that certain groups of the society conduct certain rituals and rites at the time of death for their loved ones and friends?

They believe that death is the total eradication of all existence of life, and of living; and the complete end of the total existence of all who die and are dead sleeping in their graves; period.

However, they have disregarded the truth of the Lord in that He and all that is relative to Him; is eternal, whereas there is no end to the life of the soul; not even for the ungodly and the wicked who never receive Jesus

Christ as Lord and the savior of the world; God's only Begotten Son!

Many prefer to believe that even the relationship that they might have had with the Lord is also passed on with death, whereas they will not have to answer for any of the infractions they had committed while living on the earth.

Only according to the scripture, this kind of thinking proves to be an even bigger fantasy than that of Disney World all together!

Believe me; it was more desirable that David would admonish us live gracefully in this walk of faith.

He had already spent many years of learning, leaning and depending on the Lord for all of his needs and supply.

David was a witness to the actual benefits of walking by faith, whereas God never let him down or left him to suffer lack or need of want.

He matured to walk in the faith that pleases the Lord; so to the point that God in fact says; "he's a man after my own heart!"

While so many bible readers rush to redefine the meaning in this particular 23rd number of the Psalms; it is also obvious that they have also missed the message of the faith of David in the depths of this writing.

It takes faith to believe God to point in fact that a stance can be taken to hold on to God's unchanging hand, when circumstances may appear to even suggest to you that you have been left alone all by yourself to handle the disasters of daily living among your peers, without any assistance.

Friends; Enemies; and even family members were at the helm of causing unrest to this powerful Psalmist!

The personal testimony of my life is; I have caught pure hell and much unrest on the inside of the church and on the outside in the working environment and the neighborhood where I was living; from the sinners and from the so-called saints!

To me; people were doing everything they could to push me over the edge to break the laws of the land and of God; to commit acts of violent assaults defending myself; they just would not leave me alone!

It was in these times that I came to understand what faith is and what it means to be faithful to the word of God and to the relationship that I have with God; through the times of testing, these are the lessons that I

learned.

Alike many people that I have talked with over the years, I'd wished that I could take wings and fly away somewhere and be at rest!

A secular artist wrote and recorded a song which says; "I Believe I Can Fly;" it was indeed during these times of testing, that the spirit of the Lord began to minister unto me about faith and flying as a result of faith?

Metaphorically;[Isaiah 40:31]; in faith we soar above our problems and the painful realities of living when we need to escape and not lose control of our mental faculties; choosing senseless methods of ridding ourselves of trouble heartaches and pain.

The truth is my friends; faith enables us to do on a more heightened aspect of spiritual realism; according to the natural abilities that we have already been given the ability to do!

We as human beings; were never created with wings to fly in our natural bodies; but we were given two legs and feet to walk on, whereas, even we walk in faith.

As Jesus; approached the ship out on the sea in a storm, He came walking on the water! He's God; He could have flown if He had wanted to; but flying would not teach the Apostles in the ship the faith to be applied as they walked on the earth; that kind of faith that can only please God!

Besides, He's our maker and creator; He never created us to physically take flight into the air! Although the air is very necessary for us to live here on the face of the earth; we were gravitationally grounded to live on the ground walking upright.

However through faith, we see both Enoch in the Old Testament, and Jesus in the New Testament writings of the bible take a walk across the sky and walk away from the presence of this world. That's right; they walked away! [Genesis 5:24; Act of the Apostles 1:9; Hebrews 11:5]

The greater mystery is that Jesus is seen walking where mere men of the earth just simply do not walk on a daily basis; thus He shows us a greater walk! The message is that there is an increase in our walk if we desire to do so in faith believing God without any doubt!

Moses; and the children of Israel; could have kept on journeying, walking right across the surface of the Red Sea in faith walking over the top of the water had they believed God to do so; just as Jesus walked across the water on the sea of Galilee!

But, Moses' total faith and trust in the Lord, along with God's promises to deliver them safely to the land of promise; God parted the Sea and allowed them to cross over on dry ground most of them walking; while others rode in chariots, and some rode on the backs of beast!

I know this because the bible says that they came over to the other side of the sea dry shod; no mud on their shoes nor any water to wet their shoes.

As a result of the faith that they did have that God had indeed sent this man of God to deliver them; they marched on forward into the wilderness.

The only thing they had to remind them that they had been in Egypt were the memories of their experiences and the things in which they carried away with them as they left.

When they reached the other side of the Red Sea, they had only the reality of being on the other side to suggest to them that they had actually crossed over to the other side.

They never started singing I believe I can fly; I believe I can touch the sky; when in fact their feet were touching the ground and all they needed to do was to move their feet and walk behind the leadership of Moses and Aaron in the direction of their deliverance that God had already provided for them.

Here is a fact for your mind in essence to the truth of walking; the children of Israel walked in the wilderness for Forty years, and their shoes never even wore out! Now that's the real power of walking with God!

Birds of all species and all flying insects; that were created to fly through the atmospheres of the earth in the air and even the awesome Aircrafts that mechanically fly through the air; eventually, they have to come down from the sky and rest back on the ground; even though it may be on a hill top or on a mountain top; it is still attached to the surface of the ground on the earth!

They were never created to always be in the air; on the earth what goes up; although they may take to the sky for a while, even though their ascent might have been quite high in altitude, they must descend always coming back down to the earth!

God kept the feet of the Children of Israel perpetually grounded on the earth, walking faithfully through even a forty year journey, through sand and

Psalms Twenty ~ Three

dirt, earth and all types of terrain; even though it should have only taken them approximately an 8 day journey to get to the promised land.

Though they traveled in circles passing and missing the intended destination of the promised land; the Lord faithfully kept them walking on forward, having their bodies strengthened and their shoes were kept tight; they never disintergrated into pieces.

Don't be so quick to take faith in a direction that has never been ordained for any faithful believer in the written word of God. Search the scripture; if it's not found according to the scripture; it's not of God!

Even as David was confronted with the Philistine giant Goliath; on the battle field; he didn't fly to him, nor do I believe that it was his desire to take wings and fly...

David actually ran on his feet to meet Goliath in a dual on the battle field! He used what had already been given to him naturally to obtain a spiritual victory!

In the shadow of death; David got in a hurry to use what he already had, which was not only relative to his own chosen weaponry; a slingshot and five smooth stones!

He could have even gone up on horseback; or in a chariot? But rather, he chose the same tools used when battling in the field with the sheep. He never looked for a way out; he sought the way into the battle because he not only believed that he could walk, he was already walking in faith whereas he believed that he knew that he could win the battle!

"Yea though I walk;"

I'm not going to lose a thing nor fall short because of my ability, because faith does according to what I have been given already to do. I believe that I can walk through this, too! Running through suggest that there may be great fear; however walking through strongly suggest that there is great confidence!

You Don't Scare Me!!!

"I will fear no evil;"

Fear is forbidden to reside in the heart of a champion, for the simple reason that fear is suggesting that you abandon the task at hand and find a way out of the situation.

Fear even causes one to see their own untimely demise in the face of adversity, of which seeing such an outcome of the battle that is being faced at the time is a blatant lie straight from the enemy; because the devil is afraid of any true confident believer who trusts in the Lord.

A determination should be made long before the battle occurs in our hearts that we are going to trust in the Lord until we die.

Trusting in the Lord assures that we will not die until the Lord says so anyway. So while we're facing Goliath sized challenges and deadly situations of all kinds, we will do so knowing that the Lord has the last say on the matter.

He covers us and shields us from all the fiery darts of the wicked.

He keeps us close to him; where danger dare not approach us knowing that there is no way that we could be touched nor had in derision of the evil plot of the enemy opposition against us.

The truth is that we look at evil right in the face often but without fear, doubt or worry. We believe the word of God which assures us of the Father's protection.

The word of the Lord becomes a fortress all around us in the times of trouble, while it shatters the enemy's plot into many fragmented pieces rendering it null and void.

We must speak to ourselves on a consistent basis, so as only to be reminded in the times of trouble that we will not fear. As we spend time with the Lord on a daily basis, we find that we build the storm shelters to stand there in place ready and available as the storm approaches.

We will discover that we are prepared for the storm and all that comes with it through simply declaring and decreeing that we are not going to be partaker of fear concerning our lives.

David; said; *"for thou art with me."*

He makes his confession on a consistent basis for the simple reason that he already knew that God was with him.

He is speaking of the same *"thou"* the Jesus gives a reference to in the 6th chapter of Matthew; as He taught the apostles to pray.

{*"Hallowed be "thy" name; "thy" will be done; "thy" Kingdom come}*;

The Great I Am................
Is who David is referring to in the mention of saying; {*"thou."*}

David; was very confident in knowing who God is; he could never have gone out on the battlefield with Goliath, guessing that "God" might be the God of all victories; God of the Universe and Cosmos.

Whenever we're in doubt facing a crisis of any type, let it be known that we are subject to lose from the get go!

It is one thing to be unsure of the weapons that you are going into battle with; but it is altogether a totally different thing to be unsure of the commander who sends you into battle; doubting whether or not He has your best interest at hand. Unsure if He will even step in if things began to overwhelm you.

You've got to know that you are totally protected and that there is no part of your being exposed to the will of the enemy against you.

Even the angels of the Lord are on guard concerning you, just as they were for David. [Psalms 91:11] [Exodus 23:20]

Not only did David know that the Lord was with him, he gave reason of the knowledge that he had concerning the protection of the Lord.

'Thy rod and thy staff they comfort me;"

It is not enough just to make a claim to know that the Lord is with you, you ought to be able to declare to others just how it is that you are assured of God's presence with you in whatever it is that you may face.

When it comes down to knowing that the Lord is with you, feelings and emotions simply cannot stand in the place of total confidence and total assurance.

The average persons of the churches nowadays have been found not able to quote one scripture; they have no scripture basis for being truly saved! They can't even stand to be corrected for something that they know even themselves that what they did was indeed wrong!

They fall out of the fellowship of the church and disconnect from their fellow brothers and sisters of the church angry because they had been called out on the wrong that they had willfully committed.

David knew that God was there because of the Lord's correction of him; he said; *"Thy Rod"* being interpreted to mean that your correction is ever with me.

So many have been led to believe that the Lord will just let you roam as you please; similar to the manner in which many people rear their children, allowing them to roam free even to the point in fact that they are faced with dangers of being kidnapped and at times even death.

The children are even raised now to have a voice in matters as early as 4-5 years of age! They are being taught to shun and to disregard correction; the instructions to the children and to the young people now is teaching them to live their lives to the fullest, as they are please to do so; regretting nothing that they will have ever done!

We have all lived our lives to the fullest, the only difference is that many of us had teaching that taught us to respect boundaires and to respect other people's business affairs and their property, and to keep our hands off of their possessions.

But, God has a rod of correction for which He will stop and block any faithful believer from entering into the dangers of life; with warning. [St. Luke 12:47]

After we have gone our own way and will have done our thing, we will soon realize that we are being whipped with many stripes for our disobedience.

When God put His hands to you because you have done wrong it is not because He is angered with you; but it is for your own benefit. Because He loves you, He will correct you, showing you the error of your ways.

People are walking around mad at God on a daily basis because He will not allow them to do whatever they want to do without consequences; they had been led to believe that they had the freedom to rule the world from their own little sinful platforms of rebellious defiance to the word of God; yet they profess to love God with all of their hearts mind and soul.

So many are deceived into believing that God somehow or another have left them alone without His help simply because God will not help them to disobey His word and to live against His will for their lives.

People want God to help them to go to Hell!

Actually they want God to disregard the reason that He sent His only begotten son to the earth to die for all mankind; to bring us back into atonement and redemption for the sin that had been pronounced on all mankind; since back at the Garden of Eden!

But my friend those same people seem to realize that God indeed is there on the scene to deal with them for doing wrong.

The God who indeed loves you will not let you do that which guarantees that you will spend eternity separated from Him.......

The Lord is with you; right

now!

Have you got any idea what it means for you that the Lord passionately cares for you? Our great and mighty God personally put His hand to keeping you on the right path; because He cares for His own!

Time for you to focus on the fact that you're God's on child; He knows what He wants for His own children. You're blessed and privaledged to be called the child of God; from God's on perspective.

It's not just a claim of your own; and you know this because He corrects you when you need it the most; then He loves you right back into the place of being restored through His own mercy.

You're not kicked out of the grace of God; but you are accepted into the beloved of God as the Apple of His eye.

Accept all of the God who has accepted all of you to deliver you and to make you whole! Amen..................

"Comentary on The 23rd Psalms"

Table"s Set; I'm Spirit Filled!

Thou preparest a table before me in the presence of mine enemies: Thou anointest my head with oil; my cup runneth over.
[Psalms 23:5]

Set-up to Succeed

Table ~ A PIECE OF FURNITURE WITH A FLAT TOP AND ONE OR MORE LEGS, USED FOR PLACING THINGS ON OR DOING THINGS AT; A TABLE AT WHICH PEOPLE SIT TO EAT MEALS; A RAISED FLAT SURFACE WITH A NONDOMESTIC OR OFFICE USE, E.G. ONE AT WHICH A SURGEON OPERATES OR ONE ON WHICH A PIECE OF MACHINERY RESTS; AN ARRANGEMENT OF INFORMATION OR DATA INTO COLUMNS AND ROWS OR A CONDENSED LIST; GEOGRAPHY, (SAME AS TABLELAND); ARCHITECTURE A BAND OF MASONRY OR A RECTANGULAR PANEL ON A WALL, EITHER RAISED OR DEPRESSED AND WITH ORNAMENTATION OR INSCRIPTIONS; [MUSIC] THE PART OF THE BODY OF A STRINGED INSTRUMENT THAT ACTS AS A SOUNDING BOARD; [ANATOMY] A FLAT LAYER OF BONE, ESPECIALLY EITHER ONE OF THE INNER OR OUTER SURFACES OF THE SKULL THAT ARE SEPARATED BY A MORE SPONGY BONE DIPLOË; ANCIENT HIST TABLETS ON WHICH SOME ANCIENT GREEK, ROMAN, AND HEBREW LAWS WERE INSCRIBED, OR THE LAWS THEMSELVES; {TO POSTPONE DISCUSSION OF A BILL OR MOTION UNTIL A LAT-

ER TIME}; TO REVERSE A SITUATION AND GAIN THE ADVANTAGE FROM SOMEBODY WHO HAD PREVIOUSLY HELD THE ADVANTAGE AT FIRST; TO BRIBE {PAY UNDER THE TABLE}.

David shows us the importance of keeping our focus on the Lord, being mindful that God's got our best interest at His heart always, even before the discovery of any needs have been identified as needing to be repaired of the Lord who is able to fix all things broken in our lives.

In this life; there will often be so many people who will attempt to show you exactly how much living each individual is allotted to live.

Other people will have the audacity to measure your life according to their measuring table, or ruler; but it's not about them and what they desire or don't desire for you, it's all about the plans of the Father in Heaven.

I know the thought that I think towards you, thoughts that are good and not evil, to give unto you an expected end.
[Jeremiah 29:11]

We are going to thoroughly examine the table, and what it is that God may have prepared for his children. Since from the very beginning of time; we need to recognize and to be informed that God has always had an individual plan for everyone on the face of this planet called earth that we live on.

Not one individual has been sent to live on this earth without a plan for their life; and neither has anyone been saved and washed in the precious blood of Jesus Christ for only the carnal purpose of making up God's jewels in the earth or some sort of religious bouquet of saintly flowers in God's garden.

God does things on the top in the open; on the surface where every eye can behold the final image of what has been done. God may indeed reach all of the way down on the bottom to get you up out of the depths of the valley; but what He has indeed done for you; in you; what He will do with you and even through you will be revealed on the top!

The table top is a flatted surface where things can rest and have enough space for the things to be moved around, even enough place settings for more than one individual to be seated at the table.

The table top is to be respected as being that as more of a plateau and or a stage. As God will lift us up in this life, it is not at all about having a peak experi-

ence, it's all about being placed on a plateau, whereas we are now able to reign in our new elevation as children of the Kingdom; able to bring others to the top with us.

That's right; our lives have been staged for those people who love us and support us, as well as to those who thought for sure that they had the power and the influence to bury us beneath the heaping pile of trash and gossip to which they had assigned to our names; killing and disdaining our influence.

God; reaches way down low beneath the pile of junk and the stench of filthy laid gossip and rumors to lift us to staged authority to the glorified heights of the anointing so precious and powerful, that everyone will have to acknowledge;

"this is the Lord's doing, it has been marvelous in our eyes." [Psalms 118:23]; [Matthew 21:42]

The blessing is that God is the foundation of our newly given platform of living rest. Never a need to worry at all about the bottom falling or dropping out from beneath us, as there is no failure in God!

Whenever God does a thing, it's as eternal as He is! The fortified stability of your platform is going to sustain you until the Father calls you home; and then even after you will have been gone, other's may be left behind to carry on that of which you had left behind still standing as if it had just been built up as you transitioned.

God's moves are permanent moves; this is the very reason that David is assured that the prepared table is for him!

As a result of the table being laid out for David; God promised to bring the seed; "The Begotten Son of God," out of the linage of David; preparing for the immaculate arrival of Jesus Christ to the earth!

Even though Saul and the other enemies of David; even his own son Absalom tried to kill him, his legacy and his unblemished name has been sustained even unto this very day.

Live for God, so that your own name likewise can survive the times of removal, even in your absence; God will make sure of that; just be the very best you that God has called you to be!

I had been attacked by many of the people in the churches who felt that I needed not to celebrate or to be too excited; or too appreciative for the things that the Lord had indeed done for me spiritually in my own life.

I had accomplished some

things in the Lord that I had never imagined I would be the one to do; some way or another I was always approached with a statement to the likes;"now don't be too proud of yourself, wait on others to do it!"

Only; the others, whomever ever they were supposed to be, were never getting around to celebrating me!

So through the process I came to realize that the older saints were more concentrated with the possibilities of me becoming arrogant, more-so than they were with me learning to celebrate what the Lord had done for me.

They rode me like a mad wild horse; even though there were others who were very arrogant and prideful that never seemed to catch their attention?

Nevertheless; they were affixed on me! I learned to praise God for what He had done for me in my own life; anyway!

Whenever we fail to acknowledge God by celebrating that it is the Lord who have done these things for us, we lose sight of who we not only are, but who we have become, having been transformed from who we used to be.

We stand the chance of repeating the error of who we used to be, if we allow ourselves and others to block the celebration of the new us; going back is not an option!

Who I used to be was not even good enough for me to celebrate back then; why in the name of the Lord would I stand the chance of being turned back into that direction when God is up front; up here; right now in front of me!

We are made for the glory of God; it is His assigned purpose that daily we live our lives in the manner that point us back to the Father's will and purpose for us being here in this space and time of our existence.

As each day come and go, we are given time in our natural bodies to do what pleases the Father and causes others to see His glory working in and through our lives, openly as confessing, born again believers.

It must be our intentions for the others who look on us to see the glory of God shining through us, as we work the word of God by design, carefully choosing to live according to the written word of God.

Let your light so shine before men, that they may see your good works, and glorify your Father, which is in heaven.
[Matthew 5:16]

David says; "thou preparest" ~ meaning that God never leaves

Verse ~ Five

us without provision. Consistently He provides for us on a minute by minute basis; which then becomes hour by hour; day by day; week by week; month by month; year by year; and ultimately season by season!

We're on a right now basis with God, whereas you will never find yourselves going back in time; of which is not even possible; to retrieve a blessing or any provision that the Lord had prepared for you! Get it; right now!

There is never a time or moment found in chronos; in the chronological order of things; that we will discover that the Lord had slipped or had failed to provide for us; God is ahead of us; perpetually.

To think in such a manner, is outright failure to be centered on the truth that God provides, even before we have been led to the provision after discovering any need. Jesus teaches us;

for your Father knoweth what things ye have need of, before ye ask of Him.
[Matthew 6:8 B]

The shepherd only leads the sheep to the provision where the Lord will have already prepared for us; since He already knew that we were coming to dine with Him.

We find the Psalmist/Shepherd; praising and worshipping our Lord having found the Lord to be an ever present help at all times in generality and in the times of our most desperate needs.

I have found it to be the determination of many to recognize that God has prepared for us when they are attempting to show their enemies that they are wrong concerning them; in those momentous times that they are determined to show that God had forsaken them or that He may have been punishing them for a sinful infraction from their past behavior.

It is often the mindset of the ungodly people of our society to show or to convince believers that God doesn't work that way anymore, and that it would be better to turn to the methods of the society for our provisions.

Blessed is the man that walketh not in the counsel of the ungodly. [Psalms 1:1]

We are seeing nowadays, that many of the churches are getting into deep trouble for turning to the Government for the financial need of the churches; they are being strong-armed by the government to do that which is against the word of God, and to reframe from following after the written word of God.

Many of the leaders today failed to be reminded of the fact that for His own the Lord provides! He doesn't need for any entity of the land to provide for the church.

The provisions are already in place for the need of the churches; however greed is not going to be provided for!

The hand of God will not be twisted to support selfish agendas and greed that does not even reflect the will and the purpose of God in Christ Jesus.

Perhaps your enemies; if they are in fact battling against you concerning your own selfish agenda for the people and the finances of the churches; may have a point.

However, in defense of the churches, there are those individuals who are determined to never give the church a copper penny; they are often the ones who have much to say about what the church ought to do with the finances of the churches faithful financial supporters.

Through our obedience to the scripture; we are able to tell the people of the society to step off and to be seated away from the business of the churches; as long as we are not breaking any laws as mandated by the state legislation, concerning our taxable status.

We know our place and how to stay in it! Jesus; is still and forever Lord of the churches; even the Head of the churches; many who are indeed faithless had taken the helm of the churches and cannot see the provisions of the Lord for the churches.

It takes faith assured, to be able to look into the realm of the spirit through prayer and fasting, to see where the hand of the Lord is concerning the church.

Faithlessness does not only render the leadership as blind; but they are also dead to the will and to the purpose of the Lord concerning the church.

Many, of today's leaders are stooped low-down to the ground; they are crooked and bent over; often overwhelmed and stressed to the maximum to produce for the church that which only should be manifested through the spirit of the Lord.

The leaders are high-strung and totally self-indulged with being the one on the platform, right out in the front of the people who come in attendance of their churches; which are by the way not even ministries? Many of the churches are incapable of ministering to the spiritual needs of the people who attend.

The church had always been setup and established by God to attend to the needs of the people; it was the spirit of the churches in so many words to say; what can we do for you?

Nowadays; the churches are demanding of the people, saying to them; what can you do for your church? Why are you even here? The worth and the very value of the people of the churches are being determined by the amount of their tithe and offering.

The callings and their spiritual gifts are being totally overlooked and most often disregarded; especially when their financial support is not up to par, according to that particualar ministry.

Many who are truly gifted and anointed by God are being set aside in the corners, and asked to be silent; or they are subtly being placed in insignificant man-made organizations within the churches that cater to the more carnal side of people, with the hopes they will eventually die spiritually on the inside of themselves.

As long as they are seeking God and spiritually walking in the anointing, they are a detriment to the selfish agendas of the wrong church; but they are weapons against the devil; the ultimate enemy of all of the churches of God; so they should be encouraged to keep walking with the Lord.

Many of the churches are now adamant about having the people to come out to the churches to play games that entertain the minds of the people, so as to get their minds off of their problems and situations.

They have developed sociable humanistic methods of settling the people down into groups that identify them with each other per their problematic status.

People who have financial woes and credit problems are being pushed aside as being incapable of influencing other people around the church?

They may indeed be very spiritual people; but being spiritual is not the direction the leadership is trying to lead the people in around the churches.

It used to be that the sinners and the ungodly people on the outside of the churches made light of the spiritual warfare of the people of the churches, but now it is the leadership of the churches who make light of the people in the pews who are being processed to walk in true faith and deliverance.

Those who are struggling as a result of walking in faith or even being processed to learn to walk in faith through the spirit of the Lord, are not often received as good examples of up front leaders to show the new comers

the faith in God through Jesus Christ; the value of staying with the church, and the benefit of growing strong in the spirit of the Lord as a result of being vigorously tested and tried.

David was tested and tried on many occasions; which turned out to be of great spiritual benefit to him.

Being forced to be alone all by himself; David explored the hidden mysteries of God, whereas he was allowed the discovery of the Lord's provision to strengthen him, making him swift on his feet and quick and accurate with his own hands.

The skills of David were heightened to the maximum level beyond all that would be recognized as being normal human abilities. As the Lord guided David in the fields, he also discovered that the Lord had also provided for him on the journey.

The tables that are prepared by the Lord are firstly determined by the enemies that any individual might have to face; with consideration of the fact that the very next confrontation with an enemy will be of a totally different sort!

As we grow from faith to faith and from the diverse trials on all levels, it is soon realized that we were not all plagued with having the very same enemies to try us at every trial, with the exception of having Satan; the ultimate enemy of every believer.

Remember; [Matthew 6:8 B]; our Father in heaven, He knows what things that we have need of, because He always know who and what our enemy oppositions are!

We have been taught, first the natural then the spiritual! [1 Corinthians 15:46] That's in order, however so many people get halted at the very thought of the natural enemies who are touching us in the most physical ways.

It becomes too easy to lose sight of the spiritual provisions of the Lord when the enemies of our natural surroundings and of our bodies are wreaking havoc on us, and causing us major unrest.

We are too quick in deciding that God just may be overlooking our problems and our need; though He has already promised to meet and to supply our need.

There are some people in this land of plenty who are starving and living on the streets, homeless and destitute, in much need of care; I neglect not to also acknowledge that God has already provided for us all, and there is a way out of all the trouble and the traumatic experiences that we are allowed to go through.

What we often need more than a hefty handout, is total faith and reliance upon the all true; all powerful; able God. If God can't do it, whatever it is, it's a total waste of time to pray about it or even to give time to be concerned about it. It's a dead issue!

When we are not as watchful as we ought to be, we find ourselves telling God about our enemies, as if He is not already aware of the people who are opposing us for every reason that we can think of and for all of the reasons that we can't!

Satan; wants us to feel as if God will allow our enemies to dine and to live as kings and queens in the land; while we who confess to being the children of the Lord, go hungry and ultimately suffer lack.

The problem is that we are focused on what the people of the world is doing and on what it is that they are having as result of their own ill-gotten gain.

We only look at them and think that we want what they have; but I can guarantee you that you do not want to do what they did to have the things that they have?

Too often it is only things and stuff that people desire from the Lord; all they want is what He is able to provide for them to live as comfortably as the next person; while God wants so much more for us all, than that!

Truly anointed and blood washed believers, have so much more to offer to the people of their surrounds and they are prepared to administer to them when the need arises; though it is not at all money that the people of the world are in need of?

They already have finances and great wealth, and gain; but they don't have the peace of God!

They have the big houses and property of their own, but they have to live in assisted living quarters; they can't even live at home in their houses by themselves.

They have large pantries filled to the maximum with food, but they don't even have an appetite.

They have multiple car garages filled with cars like that of a parking garage downtown, but they are unable to drive themselves for many reason!

They have everything that you and I don't in many instances; but they can't even sleep at night or in the middle of the day, for that matter; we have God in Christ Jesus!

They are so tormented and

confused, worried about their enemies and who it is that they think or believe desire to take their stuff behind their backs. They've got stuff, but they don't have the health of the believers!

They have amassed a great fortune many of them; but they are also spending small fortunes on the doctors who can never heal them of their illness. As believers, we not only have healing, but we have the healer!

God so delights in giving to those that will ask of Him; the problem with most of the people of the world is that they have already determined that they are not going to live for the Lord and to be honorable and honest according to the word of God, with their fellowman; so they have also decided against asking the Lord for anything!

They have convinced themselves that they don't want what God have to offer to them that obey Him? My friend that's a crazy assumption; as God's got everything; HE CAN DO EVERYTHING BUT FAIL!

I know that at best, it's all a façade; the real truth is that mere men are not at all capable of knowing how to tap into the things of God without faith and God's word.

What people are finding out on a consistent basis is that God is no fool, and neither is He weak in any manner.

"Thou Preparest a Table Before Me"

David said; "Thou Preparest a Table"; in other words it doesn't just happen because of whom we might have been led to believe that we are! Rather, it happens all because of who God is!

If and when God doesn't do it, it's not even going to happen for us at all; as it relates to having the things that only God; He can provide for us.

Whenever a table is laid out for us in this life; it will only have been so because the Lord spread the table with our names on it!

The Dining Table

Whenever we hear the mention of the table, what comes to mind most often is a place for us to be seated to consume the spread of delicatessens and deserts; well prepared meats and vegetables; fine wine and good coffee and beverages!

You know that people are always hungry; but unlike animals of the wild and your pets; there is so much more to us than a meal and sleep until we get hungry again.

Even pet and livestock owners; who go out of their way to develop the skill and the aptitude of their animals, take the time to do more than to just feed them. They spend so much time in development and exercise to get the very best out of them.

Since the Lord knows what is on the inside of us, He has prepared for us to be directed to the exact table of our own destiny and for the good of our purpose.

There are many tables to be considered; however the exact table has indeed been prepared for every individual.

Respectively, we reflect on the dining table, where we sit down to well prepared meals by skilled professional chefs in Five Star restaurants and Banquet Halls; at the Award Ceremonies; Wedding Receptions; and even after church fellowship dinners whenever we think of the prepared table.

We are also always mindful of our mother's cooking, filled with all of the Love that she could give to her family; and in many instances, of our father's cooking too.

God's concern for us is so much more deeply involved than just when we have our bellies filled to the point that we can concentrate, so that we can get on with the business of living and of life.

Table Of Contents

Every chapter of our lives is written in chronological order, from start to finish; from our cribs to our graves. However; God started from our finishing end in an effort to create and to establish our beginning of living on the earth with purpose.

Your purpose is determined by and through what the Lord has designed for you to complete and to finish while you're living on the face of the earth!

I have been plagued with other people trying to determine what my life will or will not be for me as if to say that they have the final word on my life.

In the table of contents, from the introduction to the conclusion, every chapter had already been finished and completed by the author and the finisher of faith; and of my life!

God; not only have the final say on my life; but, it was God who initiated the fact that anything of honorable status should be said about my life, and of the labor and of the advantages left behind because of my contributions to the Kingdom of God.

No need in worrying yourself about what others have to say about your life and the mistakes or the mishaps of your life; as

all of us must live our own lives, whereas we are all going to make mistakes and create some blunders; it's called; living!

David had Uriah's wife in an adulterous affair; found out that she had conceived as result of the affair; and had her husband Uriah; killed, being placed on the frontline in the battle.

You'd be blessed to know and to realize that there is nothing at all surprising about your life to God.

Whether you have followed the written script for your life or not, doesn't cancel out the fact that God has always had a plan and a pronounced purpose for your life.

Perhaps my friend you should consider going back to the front of the book of your life where you will find the creator, and look into the table of contents to get your life back on track.

You will find that there are still some things left unchecked, lying dormant in the past chapters of your life that can still be implemented to create a much better flow of living for you and for all of the people around your living circle that are associated to you.

You're the one who missed the spread content of the table set before you; it has never been that God in some way or another had failed you, or had left some things off!

Your haters and enemies can never see the table that has been spread for you, when you fail to approach the table.

Come and be seated in their presence; whenever you do come to your table!

Even when your greatest enemy is the enemy right between your ears; you have got to show to yourself the provision of the Lord and move forward with much empowered determination and perseverance.

Let the people talk until their mouths are broken and can't work any longer, the story of your life is complete!

David's family never knew or imagined that he was to be the King of all of Israel and Judah; they never knew that the little lad was the giant slayer; they never even knew that he was the man after God's own heart; but his story was completely written from the beginning to the end. His story and your story alike is a very true story; believe it!

The Measuring Table

God Himself; have determined just how much of living and the bourden of being alive to put on each of us.

Verse ~ Five

And let me add by saying to every reader right now; God will not put more on anyone us than what we are able to bear; that is also the truth!

I've had a lot of battles and great opposition from other people and circumstances that were not at all immediately favorable for me; but in the long run they were indeed good for me, I'm sure of that now!

For so long it seemed as if life was just so unfair to me; I could never imagine why it was that I would have to experience so much pain and heartache from such young and tender age of living; I'm sure that I thought that I was too young for that?

But as I have matured as a man and in the Lord, according to the word of God; I've come to realize that the non-desirable circumstances of my life were well mixed and measured just right for me.

I'm still here in spite of what I might have experienced and suffered at the hands of the leaders that I always thought of as being such loveable people.

Life hasn't taken me out, and neither did any of them; whomever they may be!

Not only did the Lord measure my trials and tribulation, and my pains of living; He measured the grace and favor to sustain me through it all!

People are blowing their brains out, committing suicide, taking their own lives for the reason of the fact that they are determined in their own minds that living this life of theirs is too much?

The truth just well may be that God never provided for them to struggle with all of the things that they had acquired by any means necessary.

Many people will cut your throat and stab you in the back just to have what they want, while others will go as far as to kill you and to take what you have so that they can live like you do?

They have their own measuring table for others; they think anyway. No need to worry about other people trying to deny you of the quality of living that you prefer; seek the Lord to see and to know if He has also provided that style of living for you in this life.

The Operating Table

You know that if it were not for the Lord on our side, many of us would be dead already.

Only God knows for sure of the many sickness and diseases that made an attempt to try and

fall upon you that were denied and blocked by His own hand of mercy and protection.

As it is; it was only God's hand in the womb, shaping you and forming your individual body, putting everything into the exact place just right adding your hair, and the color of your eyes; He did it all by Himself; on His operating table. This truth will anger some as other's were born deformed, and twisted.

The truth is that God worked and operated on each of us even before we ever thought that we would ever need a physician because of an illness.

Should you suffer an illness, you might soon discover that there are people that you thought loved and cared for you; that have been around you for years, they will not even lift one prayer for you.

They would prefer that your funeral be the next big thing of the community to take place.

So as a result, God has provided that you and I never have to rely on any of those people that we are not sure of; as God is the only one that we can trust.

It is better to trust in God, than to put confidence in man. [Psalms 118:8]

The surgeon's scalpel; when in the hands of the wrong individual is definitely deadly; though they may be skilled at using the sharp instrument.

Their heart may be filled with utter darkness, whereas they feel the need to cut somebody to their inner-core, just to see them bleed to death.

Our problem is that we levy our trust upon the wrong people the very moment that we are in need.

The wrong people have been waiting on the right opportunity to do you in; of which that opportunity is made available to them the moment you arrived with your need at the center of your own attention.

Of course David came to King Saul at the point of the need of the armies of Israel; as soon as David proved himself to the King and to the Armies of Israel; the King's heart turned and was sickened to the point that he wanted to kill David!

David did what none of the trained warriors of the army of Israel did not; but they could not do!

If it had not been for the Lord on His side...

Whether you need people or they in fact need you, it pays to be watchful and to pray because people are surely subject to change on a moment's notice.

I have lived this scenario

enough to tell you that you and I should have been looking to the Lord for what we needed!

Some people need desperately to see you in dire situations; they need to be able to tell you that they can't help you; when in actuality the truth is that they are not going to help you even though they are able to do so, and it would never affect their own flow of living.

There are some people that need desperately to tell you no! They need to think and to believe that their foot has been placed just right on your neck; you're down and could never get back up!

That makes them to feel so much better about where it is that they think that you are; you're still beneath them sociably; they think anyway!

"Before Me"

David is in the spirit of rejoicing, upon realizing that the table that has been prepared and spread; it had all been done just for him. He had the best seat at the table; possibly the only seat at the table?

Well thought of; well prepared; well put together having the best interest and the best plans, all laid out on the table, set and prepared just for him.

There comes a time in life when it doesn't matter what everyone else is getting, the excitement is all about what it is that I am receiving; it's my time to be blessed. YES!!!!!!!!!

David makes this statement; *"thou preparest a table before me"* ~ this statement suggest that he realized that the Lord had not forgotten all about him.

It is so important to realize that you have not been overlooked, but it is even more exciting to see the manifested results of the Lord's care for you.

It's to the likeness of the woman who receives the beautiful bouquet of roses; upon receiving them she says to the person presenting them to her; "this is all for me!"

The celebration is in order, it's totally okay to lose it for a few moments with the joy of excitement for being so well thought of.

Have you ever seen the graduate student receive the keys to a new car; upon graduating they seem crazy with excitement after haven received their diploma; then they receive the unexpected keys to a brand new car?

Can you remember how they lost it with all of the excitement?

How about seeing an homeless parent receive the keys to

their brand new home; paid in full! If the Lord says the same, they will never be homeless ever again.

The inescapable element here in the topic of discussion that David had to deal with, were the enemies.

While it would be ideal to avoid any discussion of enemies; the truth is that everybody has got an enemy or enemies.

Often the excitement is heightened relative to the fact that there has been those persons who are ever present, circling around our atmosphere, driving up and down the street where we live, showing up at the church where we attend to worship God, and as fate would have it at times they even show up at the very same restaurants that we choose for a particular dining experience.

We are consistently annoyed allowing ourselves to feel as if there will be nothing specially unique for us, in that it appear that all of our enemies are having what we are having but only at a greater measure.

Then of course our enemies might just be able to enjoy the pleasures of living that have not been awarded to us for any number of reasons.

To receive blessings with your name on it without a doubt sends a shiver up your spine and a sense of appreciation that you could have never ever imagined would emanate from your being.

Others will soon know what it is that has got you praising God in the way that you are! I'm talking about the kinds of blessings that will have you singing; "I've got praise and I've got to get it out!"

There is a much different kind of praise that comes from an individual who has been assured by way of receiving the blessing that was intended just for them.

You might want to consider the fact that God know some things about your enemies that you could never know about them!

He knows why your table must be spread right before you; laid out in your presence firstly.

"In The Face Of My Enemies"

God need to bless us in the presence of our enemies! This being the reason that God has never intended for us as the children of the Lord to be consistently on the run, fleeing the presence of the people who wish us ill!

It has become the determination of the body of Christ's society, to prove to the world that they are wrong about the Lord; when all it takes is for us all to be as Moses instructed to the Children of Israel; "Be Still!"

Not at all meaning for us to stand there in our place of position in the Lord incapacitated and motionless! And neither is this a command suggesting that we cease to complete the work assigned to our hands that we have been working on.

In the military and the Boy Scouts of America; the commander would say to us; "As You Were", meaning for us to continue on as we were before a command came along causing us to periodically, though momentarily, to cease our actions.

Certain actions of our enemies will have the kind of effect on us which may cause us to cease our own actions; no matter what they might be; for a moment or so; maybe as result of fear of some sort?

But God; through it all is saying to us; "AS YOU WERE!" I can hear us now enquiring of the Lord; "But What About Our Enemies?"

God's answer to us; is for us to just remain the same as we have always been in the Lord; I'm working for you; but, in their face! Leave your enemies to me!

We need to stop thinking that God is calling us to attention as result of the enemy's actions! We should already be attentive and vigilant on watch of our enemies. [1 Peter 5:8]

And never should we think that we hear the Father saing to us to be "at ease!"

While it is important never to take our enemies for granted; neither is it important for us to be fearfully overwhelmed over our enemies because God's got us!

Some people may need to realize that the only reason that it seems to be taking God so long to send that mindblowing blessing into their lives is because they refuse to "be still!"

If your enemies have the power to change your position and to drive you away; they also have the power to alter the arrival of your blessing?

This is the reason that they are always working against you; and for sure the reason that they always seem to have your name in their mouths.

God is going to bless who you are right now; as that is the individual that He has been watching all of the time; even though He will also bless you to become the greater person in your near future!

God is going to bless the you

that even you are most familiar with; not nevessarily the person of whom you are going to become! The person that you are becoming, hasn't even developed the maturity to even handle the blessing that the Lord may have instore for that new you.

Your enemies have way too much power over you if they are able to suggest that you even change on the Lord!

What you are missing is that they are subtly driving you away from all that you have been living faithfully for; and all that you have been praying and believing God to bring forth in your life by faith!

All along the Lord has been aware of the trouble that your enemies have been causing you and the unrest that you have allowed as a result.

God has the power and the authority to show all of our enemies that He is God; just as He did for Moses, and for the Children of Israel!

Alike those of us today, who are not afraid to tell our enemies that our God is all powerful; perhaps the children of Israel had the opportunities to tell their oppressors; that one day the Lord would deliver them and set them free.

It would have been common for such a statement to fall on death ears; as it often did even in the presence of Moses and Joshua; until God began to move for them!

Don't be so quick to buy into what your enemies are saying about you! There may be those times when you are defenseless against the onslaught of your enemies; that doesn't mean that you're supposed to bow down to the enemies ideas about you, and sell out to become their slave.

God has a sense of humor; I think that it's funny to God how mere men think that they have the power over God's elected people to opress them and to over power them; denying them the access to the provisions of God?

Give God the time to laugh at your enemies; He's coming to your rescue! God will mock the actions of your enemies. [Isaiah 54:17]

It's their face that God wants to see when your blessing are placed at the table with your name on it! They are already defeated, but it's you and them, whomever they may be; that need to see their defeat in the presence of the Lord!

They need to even see that what they thought they were preventing you from receiving,

was not even close to the actual blessing that God had intended for you, and did give to you!

Nobody is God; But, God!

At the table and in the presence of God; our enemies are reduced to being nothing more than distractions to knock us off of our focus, and to hinder our ability to expect our blessing from the Lord.

"Thou Anointest My Head With Oil"

Here, David is saying to us; "I can assure you that I know that it's the Lord's doing!" [Psalms 118:23]

He has placed His approval upon me; I have been endowed with the spirit of the Lord; I can now assure you because I've been assured myself!

Nothing more humiliating; could ever happen to anyone like trying to convince others of something that you said happened to you; to which you have no proof of evidence?

No matter how charismatic you might appear or how convincing you are at telling the story of your experience; if you have nothing to show for your alleged account, your story is totally null and void, and completely weightless!

God never leaves Himself; or any of us without a witness to what He has done. Once the hand of God has moved, the results can always be traced even in the realm of all humanity.

Though there may be others who refuse to acknowledge that God is God; they can never deny the works of His hand!

I hear David saying; not only am I put on the plateau of my high place of elevation; I am given the powerful authority of the spirit of the Lord to do the work that I have been chosen to do.

Not only is the table spread and set for me; but I have been justified to take my assigned seat.

When you've been anointed to do a particular assignment, there will be no one who can do your job, period.

We as people get lost all of the time focusing on the fact that others may be just as skillful and or as knowledgeable as another person, which just may be the truth; but the anointing makes all of the difference when being placed and elevated by God.

To "Anoint" ~ means to pour; therefore the anointing is the poured out presence of the Lord; into the life of an individual; with very tangible effects, when touch is made in contact with another individual.

which opens them up to the wisdom and to the knowledge of the Lord!

The anointing activates all of the gifts of God; to connect humanity with God who created us all. Things go wrong with humanity that only God can fix and restore; the anointing is God's way of stepping down to the presence of humanity to work in our favor; although He will often work through another human being.

There is no one on the face of the earth that has been anointed that God never intended for them to be anointed! It is God's intentional plans for the anointing to be levied upon an individual; it's not possible that it could ever be a mistake.

Note: The anointing is not necessarily our possession for a show to other people while we pound upon our chest like King-Kong; to prove that we have the power of God flowing through us!

It is the only manner and the full assurance of which that we who minister to God's people are able to successfully touch them at the very core of their spirit at the point of their need. Amen!

The anointing is God's kindness given to assure us that He is pleased to use us for the His glory. Whereas; the anointing equips and assures an individual of their ability to do what God has called upon them to do.

The anointing itself is not at all about the performance of any task or assignment that a person might have been assigned to do; the anointing reveals the actual truth that a person has been called of God to do what they are doing.

The anointing then becomes our hands to touch an individual; it becomes our eyes to see in the realm of the spirit where things are totally obscured to the natural ability to visualize the things in the spirit realm.

The anointing becomes our ears to hear what the spirit of God is speaking to the body of Christ; whether it is world-wide or at a local congregation; and especially whenever in the presence of an individul; one on one!

David is intent on us getting the understanding that he has been anointed with "oil." Now that we know that the anointing is the poured out presence of the Lord; the understanding of the oil adds the finishing touch to the mystery of the connectivity of man and God.

Verse ~ Five

The "Oil" ~ is indiciative to that of the spirit of God; but more-so in the likeness to the powerful flow of the spirit. The liquid-like matured release in the flow of the spirit of God. The exact likeness of God; whereas it is God that is assured this time that you are going to do exactly what He wants you to do.

The oil of God is not given to just anyone, though they may desire the oil; only the chosen can receive the oil of God's anointing. God is adamantly selective in choosing who will receive the oil of His anointing.

Many have the anointing; but others have actually received the oil of the anointing, like that of a power-booster.

Many are called, but few are chosen.
[Matthew 20:16; 22:14]

The difference is that the "Oil of the Anointing" goes "Boom" and "Bang" in the presence of God, whereas the atmosphere is totally turned inside out, and things will never be the same!

The anointing is poured out all over you; but the oil allows for the anointing on you to flow out all over the people in your presence; though the number of the people may be in essence of thousands in attendance!

All through the scripture we see the working of the anointing with oil, in the midst of the people; The prophet Samuel had been commissioned by God to anoint Saul with oil; to anoint him king over all of Israel and Judah; as the kingdom is stripped from Saul; God commissions the Prophet to anoint David as the new King of Israel. He poured out the oil onto the heads of both of them.

I would like to borrow from the miracle of feeding Five Thousand men on one occasion, and Seven Thousand on another occasion.

The true connection in all of the scenarios is Jesus Christ; The Anointing {Christ; The Anointed One!} There is no one anointed who refuse to accept Jesus Christ; as Lord and savior.

The apostles were power-packed with the anointing everywhere they went. Peter was so anointed that the people were laid out on the sidewalk of the streets on couches and or their beds, and as he passed by them when his shadow passed over them they were healed. [Acts 5:15]

But we can go back to the old testament; when a dead soldier were thrown into the grave of the prophet Elisha; the bible

reports that his bones were so anointed that the moment the dead man's body made contact with the bones of the prophet, he revived and bagan to live again. [11 Kings 13:21]

God knows that there are other people who can do what you do even better than you do; but He also knows that the other person or people are not as faithful as you are. And neither are they going to be awarded the powerful flow of His presence!

God knows when an individual will never trust another source, or go out of their way to avoid Him in the time of any trouble.

God knows who He can trust; thank God that He does not get overwhelmed at any ability that any of us might possess; He is often pleased more-so that we are surrendered to the spirit of God and by our availability to be used by Him.

We become available when we have turned our hearts to worship the Lord in spirit and in truth.

David worshipped the Lord at all times and the Lord's praises were always on his lips. [Psalms 34:1] It was in his heart to acknowledge God in every situation being careful to please the Lord being watchful to know that the Lord was indeed pleased with him.

It is the desire of many people of the churches to be uplifted and elevated by the Lord, but as soon as they get to a certain place of elevation, they are further determined to believe that now they can handle things all on their own.

The Lord knows those of us who are determined in our heart to go all of the way with Him.

The simple understanding is that whatever it took to get us to where we are, it's going to take that and then some of the exact same thing, even more-so now, to keep us there.

It's crazy to try and overlook the fact that you really did not have much at all to do with being where you are, other than the fact of prayer; and try to go forward without having a clue of what it even takes to be where you are.

Even though you are extremely arrogant and prideful, determined to convince other people that you are prolific and knowledgeably deserving of being where it is that you are.

The anointing keeps us focused on the fact that the Lord did it for us and that we are not our own, and we never made it on our own!

Verse ~ Five

The pure blessing of the anointing is so rich and wonderfully empowering that it constricts us, pulling us closer to the Lord's presence, constraining us to adhere to the word and to the will of the Lord for our lives, making the commitment to never ever leave the Lord's presence.

The longer we stay with the Lord, the anointing even prevent us from desiring the fellowship of the ungodly and the adamantly sinful people of our surroundings.

The anointing is extremely powerful in that it enables us to release the presence and the power of God into the atmosphere of any surrounding. The anointed people of the Lord are the true Super-Natural beings of the earth; {*not the superheroes' of the Hollywood film industry, and the cartoons*}; but the spiritually super natural individuals of the churches who are the misfits of society!

We are not at all the normal people alike most other people of the society, as we are often referred to as being weird and creepy, spooky spiritual, or just plain ole scary to the spiritually illiterate and to the unlearned; ignorant to the things of the spirit of God.

This might be a good place to stop and to be very sure to understand that no one has the power to spiritually endow themselves, which is what it means to be anointed!

Okay; now that we have that understanding, let's springboard off of the truth the we have the anointing; let's dive right into the deep end of realizing just what it is that we have been given from the Lord.

God; being the maker and the creator of all mankind; He is Spirit; therefore God will use your hands and my hands as conduits of the power of God to connect other people not only to the power, but to the power source!

God; being the source; He empowers us to become the actual witnesses to His power with undeniable evidence. God uses us to get the message over to the people of the earth assuring them that;"He Is God!"

It often saddens my heart to see people on the streets of certain big cities, dressed and donned as the superheroes of the large screen films, walking around for the purpose of entertainment keeping the people in mind of the movie and cartoon characters. But denying the power and the present reality of God in Christ Jesus.

You get the feeling that they dressed themselves as these characters simply because they believed in the film industries depiction of the superheroes; as we see them go all out to portray the characters fictitious roles of behavior.

Some have even engaged themselves in physical combat with real live people on the streets only to come up quite short of being heroic battle giants of victory; they lost the fights on the streets!

The superb spirit of the Lord's extra essential subsistence; is applied to our natural being, whereas we are now capable of doing those things of the spirit of which would be otherwise, totally impossible for us to do.

Our hands become spiritually transformed to be the Lord's hands, though they are yet natural, the spirit of the Lord flows unrestricted though our hands.

We can now outwardly touch a natural man with our hands, but simultaneously we are reaching inwardly to touch the spirit-man on the inside of an individual that we of our own natural abilities are forever incapable of doing without the spirit spirit of the Lord on the inside of us through the anointing making this possible.

The activated anointing of the Lord becomes our navigational system of mobility and travel, and our compass leading us always accurately in the actual direction to do what has been assigned to us by the Lord.

The awesomeness of God knows who, what, when, how and where it is that we are needed to be used of the Lord; not only has the Lord equipped us to do a certain thing, but He directs us in every way that is needed for the task.

The endowment of the anointing transforms our natural abilities to become spiritual tools and even when needed, weapons against the enemy.

So often we need to see beyond the surface and behind the façade of performances of the people in the religious communities who have never been transformed by the renewing of their minds, but they know how to act the part!

Through the anointing we are enabled to spiritually connect with other children of the Lord no matter what continent they may live on, and it doesn't matter of their status.

Every leader in the Kingdom of God needs to be endowed with the spirit of the Lord; there would be much less scams and

deceptive disorder happening to the people around the churches.

Being anointed; David stopped Goliath in his tracks; no situation or person is too big to be handled when faced with the anointing.

"My Cup Runneth Over"

It is for a truth, that multiples of people have experienced the touch of the Lord's own hand.

But, just knowing that at one time or another in an individual's life, that a touch from the Lord had been received, is insufficient because one is suggestion that the Lord came to them at one time in their lives, but He left as soon as He came to them; and they are satisfied with that, as if to suggest that the spirit of the Lord is now lying dormant inside of them!

God has promised to never leave us nor to ever forsake us; but it is our responsibility to ensure that He is welcomed and pleased to live with us consistently.

Most of us have better sense of reverence for the need to prepare ourselves for the trips that we are about to take; we know the necessity to fill up the tank of the car to the point that it is even full, though we may have to stop on the way to refill the tank again, thank God that we made it to that point!

Just because we had put gas in the tank of the car on last week would not be sufficient for the journey that is upon us right now; new measures must be taken to refill the tank.

Erroneously; we compare our spirits to automobiles; and we compare to spirit of the Lord to that of fuels that burn for sure, but they have tendency to burn up and to burn out. The spirit of the Lord is everlasting!

Too many of the leaders are rigorously fighting against being filled with the Holy Ghost! They want to do the work of the Lord but without the Lord's spirit on the inside of them empowering them to do so.

God's work; God's way! The Lord requires those of us who lead the people of God to depart from iniquity; you will never leave that city of sin on your own.[ll Timothy 2:19]

Sin is too busy appealing to your feelings and to your own emotions; it always feel good while lying to you about the truth of your status as an iniquitous sinner, full of the devil's influence; while it is not at all the spirit of the Lord living inside of you while you lead God's people in whatever direction you are

feeling at the time!

Then there are those who are so careful as to keep the fire contained as it burns in the fire place? The only reason that you are so preoccupied with trying to contain the fire is because you fail to know that the fire of the Holy Ghost is too hot and too vast to be contained.

It will not only burn up the wood or the burning elements, but it will also burn up the container to which the fire is burning.

An utterance of tongues does not at all depict the fact that one may indeed be full of the Holy Ghost with Fire; whereas the spirit and power of God will fill the cup and it is now running over.

Here's how it works; there is one baptism of the spirit but there are many infillings; and that doesn't mean, many internal feelings about the spirit touching your emotions!

People feel a lot of things and then assign it as to that of being the Holy Ghost. That is the reason that there is one baptism that we receive, which is then settled on the inside of us where it is also permanent.

Whenever we hear a message from the word of God, and or learn scripture, it's permanently our's; especially should you remember never to forget the word of God spoken into your ears and your spirit.

There is no way that when preached, the scriptures of the word that we had received could ever burn up or burn out. The word of God is eternal; forever! It is inflamed of the fire of God!

It's permanently our's; it's a part of us now! We meditate on that word, especially when we are overwhelmed to receive the word. The word is then allowed to impact our lives whereas it actually becomes installed on the inside of us as an installed floor in a building being constructed that is to be very tall with many floors installed. The impacted word makes room for more word to be installed.

Once that word is settled in our hearts; it becomes time for another word. Thus the cup is never empty! More word is poured in; more experiences with God are poured in; more of the Love of God is poured in; and finally more of the spirit of the Lord causing the cup to over-flow!

The over-flow of the cup; is when the spirit of the Lord; on the inside of us causes us to share the word that is also richly impacted inside of us with others; alike the Prophet Jeremiah; who vowed initially that he wasn't going to tell nobody else about the Lord; but then he declares that the word of God inside of me was like fire shut in my bones; there was no way that he could contain it! It spilled over and ran out of his mouth! [Jeremiah 20:9]

It is so necessary that we as the leaders of the church not only lead the people in singing I surrender all; but we must firstly be truly surrendered and filled up and overflowing with the spirit of the Lord.

It is suggested and reported now more than ever before in the history of the church, that some leaders of the churches are too spiritual, and that they are scaring the people! Really?

This is one of the biggest lies ever told to any leader of the church, remember that God is a spirit; it's impossible to be God's man or woman, refusing to be spiritually transformed whereas there is more of God's spirit flowing from you as you lead the people, than there will ever be of yourself and the natural propensities of the flesh to commit willful sin.

David had no problem allowing others to see the light of the Lord; when your cup is running over, others, who wished that they could never see the light of the Lord shining through you, will see the light!

Whenever they are in your presence they can feel or sense the presence of the Lord flowing out of you.

God's Love is Great and Mighty; it is inescapable to those who come into the vicinity where the spirit of the Lord is allowed to flow freely and is received.

David had enough assurance of the Lord's loving spirit in his own life to share that very same assurance that the Lord loved them and that He would be the same God to them that he had been to him.

People want to be leaders of the church with authoritative power of their own personal flare and influence, while they are in desperate need of being leaders with the overflowing fire of God's Love.

As it is, many people of the churches have been influenced, but they have not all been influenced to live or to love like the Lord.

Many leaders of today fear major publicly embarrassing sexual scandals even though their sexual behavior may call for it.

Pastoral manuals and how to

leadership conferences for the ministry is not at all how one is enabled to go about the ministry blameless and free of sinful blemishes.

But; being full of the Holy Ghost will ensure that as a leader, the people under your leadership might see you at a time where you are stressed, but never drunken on alcohol or drugs; an embarrassment. [Galatians 5:16-21]

Being audited and found guilty of financial infractions by the IRS as the pastor of the church; will result in your stay in a Federal Penitentiary!

The people who were once so very proud of you, will to turn on you and leave your churches refusing to even acknowledge that they had ever even known you.

Many pastors are not at all inclined to teach the people of their churches for the sake of them growing to one day become the leader of the church themselves; their greater strategies are geared towards keeping them under their own pastoral rulership and control.

The truth is that there are more leaders alike Saul then there are alike David!

Saul fueled the conspiracy against David, alike many of the leading pastors do today; they feel the need to kill the influence of others so as to boost their own personal brand for the people to like them instead.

Sometimes in their own churches there is rumors and gossip about certain people of their ministry to which they will not assert themselves as the mediator to stop the madness of the onslaught against their follower; rather they are involved in causing the unrest and the painful slander.

David could have become everything that Saul was indeed, had it not been for the Lord filling the cup of David with His own spirit.

David admired King Saul even as you and I would probably admire the greatest leader in the land; with great desire to serve him, and he did do so.

Alike David, people need for sure to be more inclined to worship the Lord and to serve the Lord with gladness; they who have such desires of their heart will always be led to leadership that is full of the Holy Ghost.

The Love of God fills, and it rests in the atmosphere of the spirit filled churches, where the people are taught to be filled with the spirit themselves.

Look for the fruit of the spirit, not the emotional expressions of

Verse ~ Five

the people who are supposed to be under the power of the spirit, where people clap their hands and shout out aloud and run the aisles and dance in praise to the Lord.

But the fruit of the spirit is love, joy, peace, longsuffering, gentleness, goodness, faith, meekness, temperance, against such there is no law. And they that are Christ's have crucified the flesh with the affections and lust. If we live in the spirit, let us also walk in the spirit. Let us not be desirous of vain glory, provoking one another, envying one another.
[Galatians 5:22-26]

Verse Six

"Comentary on The 23rd Psalms"

For Sure; Lord I'm In Here!

Surely goodness and mercy shall follow me all the days of my life : and I will dwell in the house of the Lord forever.
[Psalms 23:6]

"An Assured Promise"

SURELY ~ (SHOOR~LEE`) ADV. 1. WITH CONFIDENCE; UNHESITATINGLY. 2. UNDOUBTEDLY; CERTAINLY: YOU SURELY CAN'T BE SERIOUS. 3. WITHOUT FAIL: SLOWLY BUT SURELY SPRING ... ADVERB 1. FIRMLY; UNERRINGLY; WITHOUT MISSING, SLIPPING, ETC. 2. UNDOUBTEDLY, ASSUREDLY, OR CERTAINLY: THE RESULTS ARE SURELY ENCOURAGING. 3. (IN EMPHATIC UTTERANCES; COMPOUND FORMS/FORME COMPOSTE: SLOWLY BUT SURELY ADVERB: DESCRIBES A VERB, ADJECTIVE, ADVERB, OR CLAUSE FOR EXAMPLE, "COME QUICKLY," "VERY RARE," HAPPENING NOW

David the Psalmist' begins this statement with total confidence; and without a doubt he states a claim on the greater things of living and of life on the earth through the Lord our God.

Looking at this statement most bible readers have been hasty and very quick to assign it as being the common expectation of the least normal things to come being a member of the local church; not even truly considering themselves as being a spiritual child of God.

Not very many people are able to see that there is so much more than meets the eye here in this statement; but I guarantee you this declaration is loaded to the max!

Whenever we look to one side of the meaning of a word and never at the alternative side/ or the objectionable sides of the definitive composition for the conformed perplexity of any contextual basis, we are only awarded a menial reasoning for understanding the ultimate meaning of the word, when there is indeed so much more to be explored to release the total impact of the word's usage.

This is so; relative to the erroneous teachings from past teachers and instructors who were satisfied with the very first and most basic definition of the word, or words in this matter. Thus I say; Look Again!

The Lord; in His kindness, has let me in on this *matter of fact knowledge*; David came upon the knowledge of the fact that there is more to the subject matter than what is often first thought of at the first glance or at the initial mention of the matter.

This should be taken as a lesson to those of us who take out the time to investigate and to read and study the word of God. In another book earlier, I wrote a chapter titled; "READ BETWEEN THE LINES."{"Once Bitten Forever" The Tree of Knowledge of Good and Evil}

Those who are willfully surrendered to the anointing and to the will of God; only they will be able to actually grasp the unwritten data between the lines.

Through the aid of the spirit we become aware of what it is or might have been that the writer has omitted to say or to even write, on purpose.

Remember; David opened the 23rd number of Psalms here saying that; "THE LORD IS......"

When indeed you have gotten the revelation of who the Lord *is*; and that the Lord is; there is no question as to whether or not the Lord is able to share deeper revelations of the word of God with you.

Many Theologians and Sunday school teachers are often set on getting us to accept what we have read for face value; and to simply settle our mental focus on it as being the only thing that there is to possibly receive from the subject literature.

Even, as if to suggest to treasure hunters who are at a particular location knowing that there is buried treasure there; that it would not be good to dig, or don't dig, or at best it would

Verse ~ Six

be of no consequence to them if they were to dig there?

> In the beginning was the word, and the Word was with God, and the Word was God. The same was in the beginning with God. All things were made by him; and without him was not anything made that was made. And the Word was made flesh, and dwelt among us, (and we beheld his glory, the glory as of the only begotten of the Father,) full of grace and truth.
> [St. John 1:1-3; 14]

What has been lost on most of the people of the churches nowadays is the fact that God is Word; thus we have the benefit of working with the spirit of the word and for sure the word of the spirit.

God is spirit; [St. John 4:24] so we should understand that God is spiritual word; the spirit of the word; and the word of the spirit! And of course the written word is the product of the spoken word of God.

Eternally one in essence and they can never be seperated at any time. Whenever we look at God we should see the word; Whenever we look into the word we should always see God!

[Genesis 1:], Informs us of the fact that the spirit of the Lord moved; but nothing came to be until the words came out of the mouth of God telling the things which were to come what it was to be and the manner of which it was to be, and the exact location of where each thing was to be placed upon the face of the earth!

The word don't move without the spirit; But, the spirit don't move without the word! The spirit and the word they are one; so to have one without the other is a sure indication that you are incomplete.

The scriptures; too often are taken as only probable instances of natural happenstances; and some would even dare to consider the scripture as fictitious religious entertainment!

People refuse to see God and truth in the bible. Even as the spirit of the Lord said to the church at Laodicea;

> I know your works and I know that you are neither hot or cold; I wish that you were either hot or cold; but because you are lukewarm, I will spew you out of my mouth; [Revelation 3:15-16;]

People of the churches and bible readers fail to make the connection of Genesis 1; St. John 1; and Revelation 3; blinded and unable to see that God; is word in motion!

Most people read Revelation 3:15-16; and think vary carnally in their own minds of God

vomiting and regurgitating as if to have eaten a bad meal of the people that He is referring to?

However; the revelation is that God is holding us all in His mouth! From the time of which we were referred to as the Cradle Row; and others were referred to as The Sunshine Band; and or the Beginners; we were taught to sing; "He's Got The Whole World in His Hand!" And yes He does have the whole world in His hand.

It is the confessions of our faith in Jesus Christ; whereas we are washed in the precious blood of Jesus, which seperates us from the world in His hand, to the very need of being kept in the word of His mouth!

You think about this for a moment or two; how does the attention shift from your hand to your mouth, when you put something in your mouth; especially when it is not at all good to your taste buds?

But you must come to the understanding and see that God's word is in His mouth! Everything that ever happened in this world all happened as the words were spoken out of the mouth of God! From the beginning to whenever the end will be; it has already been spoken out of the mouth of God. However every thing and every individual must live according to the spoken word of God. Rebellion doesn't change nor alter what God has already spoken!

We have been made accepted in the beloved; [Ephesians 1:6] The picture here is that God has said yes concerning us, all because of Christ! As the curse of death was passed over manking in all of the earth; initially what took place was that humanity was at that time spewed out of the mouth of God!

Sin is the idea of Satan; whereas he is seeking to be in the presence of God; ever since he was cast out; sin in our lives opens a doorway for Satan to reign in our mortal bodies, thus allowing a place of residence for the devil to dwell in our presence.

Because Satan have been eternally rejected of God; when we are attemptinmg to be in the presence of the Lord having been in sin, unrepented; God has to say no to us because of the rider on the backs of our souls.

You must know and understand that God always says no to Satan! We cannot afford our selves to be in partnership with the devil because there is nothing profitable for us there; God's rejection is utterly present there in the atmosphere of the Satanic reign.

Sin sours the tasteful acceptance of us in the mouth of God! Believe me; God is holding us in His mouth! The praise and the glory of God through our worship sweetens the acceptance of our reign with Jesus Christ as our Lord and Savior.

It is then at that time whenever we are determined to allow the works of the flesh through the Satanic reign to dwell in us that God decides that we have been putrified and spoiled, and must be spewed out of His mouth!

When God makes a reference to spewing you out of His mouth because you are lukewarm; now that you have been both created out of the mouth of God in the spirit and formed from the dust of the ground having now been the seed of God's creation from the beginning; it needs desperately to be understood that God being word will have no more word to say concerning you; nothing else to say to you; and He will make no more request of you! He has nothing else to say to you; period!

He will have no more instruction for you; no more word of correction for you; and neither will He have any more word of admonition given for you, and will even cause you to lose a desire for hearing the preached word of faith and deliverance.

It rends my heart that so many people are so very comfortable being lukewarm, on a daily basis. So many have been deceived and even misinformed to think and to even believe that if they are not actively hot; living spiritual and holy that the devil will not bother them, and that they can live a trouble free life?

We all know people who live this way; refusing to actively participate in the local church or any bible studies, or Christian programming of any type.

To them this is some type of safe living in a safety net on neutral grounds, where the enemy can see that you are spiritually unarmed and absolutely no threat to the kingdom of darkness?

Be advised that that does not at all disarm the devil concerning any human being on the face of the planet!

When God have no word for you as a result of you being lukewarm; all scriptures concerning you being covered and protected by the angels of the Lord are no longer applicable to you.

For He giveth His angels charge over thee, to keep thee in all thy ways.
[Psalms 91:11]

It is a dangerous thing to live so that the Lord will remove His hand from covering you to protect you and to keep you in all of your ways!

It doesn't matter that many theologians and religious instructors will argue that this writing is out of context and in error; of which is usually the argument for everything that doesn't set well or jog with their determination of the scripture.

Such erroneous teachers of the scripture fail to believe that God Is!

God; the creator of all of Heaven and Earth; in His own infinite wisdom; creative power and authority not only said what *(it)* was to be that came out of the mouth of God {each thing spoken into existence}; but, God; is what it was and is to this very day, that came to be; out of the mouth of God!

The things spoken, came out of the inner-most; and the utter-most part of God's being, to be made manifest into something that we would be able to identify with as natural dwellers of the earth, haven been created firstly in the spirit as spiritual beings of God; later formed in the natural from the dust of the ground. [Genesis 1:26-28; 2:7;]

The power of the New Testament scriptures came about after about 400 years of silence in the earth to reveal the actuality and truth of Just who God is and the fact that He is; and to give light to all that He had done in the times past upon the earth.

To make known the mysteries of the things that He had given to us; and to all of the people alive and living, and to all that would ever live in every generation of people to come.

The Prophets and the priest had no word of admonition or instruction for the people of the earth during those 400 years; whereas being without word from the Lord or from heaven, allowed the people to be left to their own humanity and self-insufficiency; only to realize that when God don't tell us which way to go in the earth, we don't know!

Whenever God doesn't tell us how, when, or where, we will error and fail tremendously at even the simplest of things relative to our daily living and our lives on the earth.

Living is filled with many complexities and difficulties which call for the need of a greater voice of instruction and authority, which can only be found in our God.

I have heard on many occasions from the pulpits and the platforms of the teachers of the bible, instructing and suggesting to the people under their teaching and instruction, that they are not to even look too deeply into the word of God to iso-gee or even to exo-gee the word of the bible.

In other words it is often viewed as an error in understanding to see more into the word of God and or even to get more out of the word of God than what is seen at face value upon first glance.

Why it is so disturbing to these biblical instructors is a bit puzzling to me; of all people they should be of the first people to get to the very depths and to the extreme foundations at the core of the word of God from the most spiritual aspect, to extract the meat from the word to adequately feed the people of God.

God is a spirit; [St. John 4:24] That alone ought to inspire and invigorate everyone who read the word of God to seek for the very most spiritual understanding, to see just what it is that the spirit is saying to the church.

As it is nowadays, so many people are approaching the church and the Holy bible with a very grounded cycle of reasoning about God and the churches as if it was to have been something that really took place in past times; whereas the things of the church and of the bible were for the people of the earlier generations and they are no longer relative to any of the people or the churches; alive today.

Whenever a revelation from the word of God is received, it is done so by the spirit of the Lord; there is nothing at all earthly or natural about the revelations of God.

It is intended by God that we receive from the spirit, in an effort to gain better understand and revelatory comprehension into the Kingdom of God; as children of the kingdom. He has the true methodology to help us live our lives on a daily basis.

The scripture says;

"the letter killeth, but spirit giveth life."
[II Corinthians 3:6C]

God; is neither worried or otherwise fearfully concerned that people are well studied and literarily prepared to understand the grammatical usage of words and the contextual placements in sentences to build the necessary meaning for the purpose of getting the intended messages of written and well-spoken lessons.

However; understand that the things that we have come to know, are but infinite, minute, and severely minuscule to the things that God knows.

God; knows why we know the things that we have come to know; He knows how we came to be knowledgeable of the things that we now know.

God knows where the knowledge originated before you and I ever came to be in existence on the face of the earth.

So even if you are a history buff, and very astute in your studies to acquire knowledge; you need also to respect the fact that God is; before any knowledge ever was; He is God!

We arrive to this point in fact that David makes such a declarative statement in this sixth verse, saying; *"surely goodness and mercy"* for which the anointed psalmist should not be taken for granted or treated as if he had been illiterate, and void of understanding seriously overwhelmed and stricken within to just say something; anything; just because, with no meaning.

Unlike many of the people of the churches today who have acquired a lot of information; only to reveal in the time of trouble and of a crisis, that they have neither learned nor do they have the knowledge of God for the sake of getting through their trials and tribulation, and most of their hard times.

For I bear them record that they have a zeal of God, but not according to knowledge. [Romans 10:3]

The Apostle Paul; alike many people in the world that will go where they know that the people of God can be found; usually at a place where they feel that the spirit of the Lord might be flowing with Love and the power to deliver their arrested souls; he travels to the presence of the Israelites.

Paul; believed in his own heart and spirit that these are the people of God; only to discover that they talk a good talk and that they are very religiously observant of religious customs; of holy days; and the laws of the religious society; but according to God who had been revealed to Paul; they did not know God at all!

David; without a doubt, he knew the Lord God; by His spirit and truth! Knowing that the Lord is, David understands that anything that comes from God is always above and beyond anything that is found on the earth; God is greater!

Mind you my friend, that this

Verse ~ Six

is not just merely a common since of goodness and mercy; but it is indeed surely absolute goodness and surely absolute mercy! Surely; He is God!

With total confidence, undoubtingly, never a question about it; He is God! [Hebrews 11:6]

David is set on getting us to understand that this is a much greater measure of goodness and of mercy handed down to us as the children of the Lord; because it's God's goodness and God's mercy!

God cares; for His own children of the Kingdom; those who call upon the name of the Lord from their hearts and that's without a doubt!

Jesus taught us on many occasions that the Father gives good gifts to His children that ask of Him, remember He says to the apostles and to the Jews standing around as He puts forth a parable;

"you being evil knoweth how to give unto your children good gifts; how much more will your Father which is in Heaven give good gifts to those who ask of Him? [St. Matthew 6:8; 7:7-11;]"
[Romans 8:15] [II Corinthians 6:18]
[1 Peter 1:17]

David; was assured that goodness and mercy would never wear out or go bad in any way. These gifts from God were to be thought of as being everlasting and untouchable as He is; as long as God lives never would Satan be able to get his hands onto the goodness and the mercy of the Lord; to prevent it or to turn it against us to work adversely; the things of the Lord they are immutable and incorruptible.

For all the promises of God in Him are yea, and in Him amen, unto the glory of God by us.   *[II Corinthians 1:20]*

Of the more assured ways to know that you indeed have things that came from God; is to be able to see that God's attributes are all over those things, intermingled in and throughout those things.

Those things will work to ensure that you are abiding in the vine and standing right in the middle of the will of God.

You will never ascertain these revealed benefits of God; to take hold of them for a possession and a blessing, until you are found and fashioned as a son of God; in Him!

"Shall Follow Me"

FOLLOW ~ VERB TRANSITIVE OR INTRANSITIVE ~ 1. TO COME AFTER SOMEBODY OR SOMETHING IN POSITION, TIME, OR SEQUENCE; OR SUCCESSION 2. TO ADD TO SOMETHING AL-

READY DONE BY DOING SOMETHING ELSE, USUALLY A RELATED THING; 3. TO TAKE THE SAME ROUTE BEHIND ANOTHER PERSON, E.G. BY WALKING DOWN THE STREET OR DRIVING ALONG THE SAME ROAD, DELIBERATELY OR BY CHANCE; 4. TO HAVE SOMEBODY'S MOVEMENTS UNDER CONSTANT SURVEILLANCE; 5. TO WATCH, OBSERVE, OR PAY CLOSE ATTENTION TO SOMEBODY OR SOMETHING; 6. TO GO ALONG SOMETHING SUCH AS A ROAD OR PATH; 7. TO TAKE THE SAME COURSE OR GO IN THE SAME DIRECTION AS SOMETHING ELSE; 9. TO ACT IN ACCORDANCE WITH SOMETHING, ESPECIALLY WITH INSTRUCTIONS OR DIRECTIONS GIVEN BY SOMEBODY ELSE;; 14. TO KEEP INFORMED ABOUT OR UP TO DATE WITH THE PROGRESS OF SOMETHING; 15. TO BE ABOUT SOMEBODY OR SOMETHING, ESPECIALLY TO DESCRIBE OR DEPICT WHAT HAPPENS TO SOMEBODY OR SOMETHING OVER A PERIOD OF TIME; 16. TO HAPPEN AFTER AND AS A RESULT OF SOMETHING ELSE; {TRANSITIVE ~ ADJECTIVE 1. GRAMMAR. HAVING THE NATURE OF A TRANSITIVE VERB. 2. CHARACTERIZED BY OR INVOLVING TRANSITION; TRANSITIONAL; INTERMEDIATE. 3. PASSING OVER TO OR AFFECTING ...} {FIRST, IT IS AN ACTION VERB, EXPRESSING A DOABLE ACTIVITY ...}

Cast not away therefore your confidence, which hath great recompense of reward. For ye have need of patience, that, after ye have done the will of God, ye might receive the promise.
[Hebrews 10:35-36]

What comes to my mind is the reasonable fact of understanding that, "after; only always comes after!"

The power transitional form of this particular portion of the statement is that it is predicated on knowing who God is to me and of whom it is that I am to Him!

In other words; it's all about the relationship developed along the way while walking with the Lord. One of the greater stresses of living is often the unknown factor of what it is that is coming up next!

We don't know most often, and for that reason alone we are often in the zone of over-ride, heavy laden with fear of the unknown.

The Psalmist steadfastly assures us of that which is to follow in succession to discovering the truth and reality about God; surrendering to His will and to His way in full obedience to His word; we are awarded the reasonable right to know just what will follow after that we will have done the will of the Father.

The greatest pleasure to assure us that we are indeed serving the Lord comes to us in full measure and then some, but not until God has been pleased that we have fulfilled the requirement of His will for our lives, according to His word.

It is in extreme error to go about in and throughout the kingdom of God and the body of Christ thinking and feeling as if we have the power to manipulate God to hurry up and to bring that which had been promised to us at the end of fulfilling His will; especially because we have grown weary of waiting.

It is necessary to become better bible scholars, because some will preach and teach any and everything that will sound good to your ears just to get you to be more comfortable in their churches.

Only; when you make earnest attempts to practically apply the methodology delivered to you in the messages, will you discover that they are empty and void of God's response to your obedience to what you had been taught, because it was in error.

Don't be so quick to hear that God needs you for any reason at all; God chooses us we do not choose Him as many are being led to believe.

All of the limits are on humanity and they are never on God at any time; I will say this again without an apology; "God can do everything but fail!"

Erroneously, many people are teaching in some of the churches that other people are running off with your blessings for any number of reasons?

David said that Goodness and mercy shall follow me!

Notice that he intentionally said me; it had been revealed and assured to him that these blessings were indeed coming to him, for him, and yes they were intentionally assigned for his own benefit.

Most people in the churches are consistently prodded and advised that it is more noble of them to pray for others and not to be selfish in praying so much for themselves?

I pose this question to you; how is it then that you are going to touch God concerning yourself and please Him to the point that He will intentionally send a blessing to you, when you are not even faithful and prayerful enough to be in expectation for any blessing concerning you?

Psalms Twenty ~ Three

....ye have not because ye ask not.
[James 4:2D]

For sure you are going to miss that blessing that is solely intended for you! It is religious jargon to think and to believe that you are doing such a favorable deed for God in praying for other people, especially whenever they will not even pray for themselves!

My friends; it's personal with God; no one is really going to be able to go before God on your behalf when you will not even go.

The prophet Samuel went down on his face before the Lord for King Saul; King Saul had been spewd out of the mouth of God; absolutely no word for the King! [1 Samuel 28:6]

The Lord said to Samuel; *"how long are you going to mourn for Saul seeing that I have rejected him?* [1 Samuel 16:1]

Alike Saul; many people are going to disobey God and go on about their business as if they had never done anything wrong!

In today's world, people behave like this because they think that they have your assurance that you are covering them in prayer so they are safe; they think anyway?

David was a dedicated worshipper, to which God knew that he was indeed! He relied upon his own relationship with the Father; not allowing anyone else to worship God in his stead.

There are things that the Father in heaven will only say to you about you! He will not even speak to the prophets concerning you, if you trust in Him and maintain a right relationship with Him; He will only tell you.

That which God will release as result of my obedience to His will, is sent in my direction with my name on it, God knows who I am without fail or any type of a mistake.

Several years back a song was written that has also been sung in many of the churches, which says; "What God Has For Me, It Is For Me!"

Think with me for a moment; every individual have their own unique set of finger prints; even though there are those people who were all born at only minute intervals of each other, sometimes in multiples of as many as eight babies, and more?

I am not at all sure as to the largest number of the most children born to one mother at the same birth; but I do know that there have been many born on the same day to one mother.

God is yet wise enough to ensure that each child has its own

identity even though all of the children born may share the exact same facial features; they look alike! They all have the same face!

So what is it my friend that could ever allow you to think that God just might get you mixed up with another person in the church or in the body of Christ?

Your spiritual DNA is greater and more assuredly identifying than your natural DNA or your finger prints.

How could God miss you when God sees things that you and I never could see with our natural vision or even in the spiritual realm without His help?

God knows things about our physical address that you and I are yet to find out; for an instance, your house may be built on the top of a gold mine; but unless He allows you to be informed of the fact you will never ever know it.

Or your house may have been built on the top of some type of an ancient burial site?

Whatever it is, God knows everything about everything that there is to know!

God knows more about forgetting than you and I could ever even become knowledgeable about remembering.

Most dedicated theologians are but at best religious anthropologist, in that their studies are after all based and ultimately affixed and founded upon the existence and the behavior of mankind in a God ordained system; as they find it utterly impossible to actually study and to figure out God.

God is to be received, as He is too vast and finite to be perceived even to the greatest IQ in the laboratory.

"All The Days of My Life"

The total assurance that David had was relative to the fact that God Is! It must be founded and settled in your heart and your total being that God is everlasting; meaning that God is forever!

Isn't it disappointing to think of the blessings of the Lord as being only a temporary fix, in what has the possibilities of being a permanent situation?

So many people are taught that when God does a thing that it may only last for a season and that you will need the Lord again; but for the very same thing.

David is still talking about this same goodness and mercy of God, that is going to last him for all the days of his life!

Psalms Twenty ~ Three

All the days of your life, can only mean some of the days of your life, if you only count the days since this truth had been revealed to you, then of course the former days didn't matter.

The moment that we enter into the right relationship with the Lord, is when all things are changed and totally rearranged for the will of God to take precedence over our lives. Remember that after only comes after; not before and neither during the present time at hand.

All of our days are numbered and set. We should have been living for the Lord from the beginning of our lives; but by God's grace and mercy we were allowed a second chance to make our lives right with the Lord; through the saving sacrifice of our Lord Jesus the Christ; the Only Begotten, Son of God!

It would be futile to spend the rest of our days concerned with the number of days that we actually have left.

We would all soon realize that we had wasted too much time attempting to delve into the mind of God to know that which even the most endeared of our Father in Heaven, can never know except He reveals it.

The real true blessing is that this promise was not only made to David; but to those of us who are joint heirs to the promise with Jesus.

We miss the fact that the promises of God are in effect in and over our lives, simply because we confuse the process of our making for the benefit and the success of our ministries, to that of having been forsaken and forgotten about by God.

Such utterly chaotic rhythms of our mindset are only going to cause any child of God to abort their own mission and purpose, thinking that it is not at all worth it?

The now late Andre Crouch wrote a song many years ago which says; "It Will Be Worth It All, When I See Jesus!" And while that is the truth, the fact is that it is worth it all right now!

We must be faithful enough to continue on through the process even when we cannot trace the hand of God, where it is not at all made plain to us what indeed the Lord is doing with us.

I have lived with God long enough now to know that God always knows what He is doing; and He knows what He is doing with me!

God knows what He is doing with all of us on the face of the planet!

Too many people are now in

the churches looking outwardly to the world's sociable aids although they claim to be seeking the Lord for what is going on with their lives.

The fact is that there is more people that are simply members with the people of the local congregation of churches world wide, more so than there are actually truly blood-washed children of the Lord who are Holy Ghost filled!

Just because you say that God lives in you, doesn't make it to be so when there is firstly no word on the inside of you, and you have purposefully avoided the infilling of the Holy ghost.

Only God can truly declare that God lives in you, as the Holy Ghost testifies for Him;

> Even the spirit of truth; whom the world cannot receive; because it seeth him not; but ye know him; for he dwelleth with you, and shall be with you. But when the comforter is come, whom I shall send unto you from the Father, even the spirit of truth, which proceedeth from the Father, he shall testify of me: and ye shall bear witness, because ye have been with me from the beginning. [St. John 14:17; 15: 26-27;]

The true power of your testimony that God lives on the inside of you is not only relative to your own mouth speaking your native language, and not even because you are consistently quoting scriptures.

Others will truly be convinced that the spirit of God dwells on the inside of you as according to the scriptures, the spirit of the Lord can and will speak up for Himself.

I urge you to be sure that it is the spirit of the Lord living on the inside of you, not for show so that other people can see it; but because if you are alike myself, I want every blessing that the Lord have in store for me!

"And I Will Dwell In the House of The Lord; Forever!"

"And" ~ is a conjunction; it has the ability to hook up words to make phrases and clauses for more pronounced sentences; it also have the power to create addendums to legal contracts that the lighter matter might become more weightier in matter for the benefit of either party in the contractual agreement.

So David creates an addendum to the promise by revelation from the Lord; as he had already been told that goodness and mercy would follow him all the days of his life; that's in the natural while here on the earth.

So he adds the eternal bliss of

the Father to the promise and he says; "and I will dwell in the house of the Lord; Forever!"

He was blessed to realize that more benefits comes with the promise than just the promise alone with God. John quoted Jesus as having said;

> "the thief cometh not but for to kill' to steal' and to destroy. But I am come that they might have life and that they may have it more abundantly.
> [St. John 10:10]

The promise here is abundant life; but Jesus substantiates the promise by adding that life would be even more abundantly; even more than at first mentioned of the promised!

The Apostle Paul; later picks up on the weightier matter of the promise and he says it like this;

> "Now unto Him that is able to do, exceeding abundantly; above all that we ask or think, according to the power that worketh in us. Unto him be glory in the church by Christ Jesus throughout all ages, world without end. Amen'.
> [Ephesians 3:20-21;]

All we will ever need in effort to know the weight of what God said is Faith in the scripture and prayer to open us up to the Father that we might receive revelation of the promise in full measure.

This particular heavily weighted number of the Psalms has been so misquoted and mishandled by so many for so many years simply because according to their own reading skill they are able to know what God said; but are unable lacking the aid of the spirit to know what God is saying; of which is often more weightier that what is written on the pages.

How many times have you ever sent a message to someone and sent along with the message the instructions for the person who receives the message that you would tell them everything when you see them at a later time?

Sometimes, for unspecified reasons, the message is left incomplete or only partially delivered; so it becomes necessary for the completeness of the message to be given in effort to shift the weight in essence to make plain the promise in the message. Again the Apostle Paul tells us;

> "For we know in part, and we prophesy in part. But when that which is perfect is come, then that which is in part shall be done away.
> [1 Corinthians 13: 9-10]

We must partner with God to deliver to the people what the full measure of God's word is saying to us all.

Verse ~ Six

So many of us are determined to go to Heaven to be with the Father when we die; thus being the only reason that many people confess to being saved; of course others are determined that they are not going to hell!

This is true and the truth; as the scripture declares that we shall ever be with the Lord in Heaven when we are no longer in the earth, as the ungodly and unbelieving will have their part in the lake of fire and brimstone, eternally separated from God the Father in heaven. [Revelation 21:8]

And I do believe that I'm going to Heaven when I am no longer in this body; amen. Do You believe that you're going to Heaven?

In an effort to get to the true understanding of what it means right now to dwell in the house of the Lord forever; there need to be a definitive comprehension of the word "FOREVER."

It might help you to understand that forever in its truest definition have no beginning or and ending. So when does forever begin?

And for certain we are never awarded an actual point of stoppage as to whenever FOREVER would or if it could ever end!

Again David said; 'THE LORD IS"… He the Lord is ever present; with us and without us! The greatest definitive aid of being able to comprehend forever will be realized whenever we look to God in the total essence of His existence; knowing that He is eternal.

I say with much boldness and confidence that forever is also better received when it is understood to be eternal; as there is absolutely no place in the earth or in the cronos of time where forever can be found!

Even the thought of forever is readily washed out and psychologically erased in the reality of all that is temporal on the earth!

Everything and everybody on the earth have but limited time span to exist on the earth, as all things that were begun, began with an end in sight, and could never be respected as being forever, or eternal.

We fail to intellectually grasp that there was a starting point with an installed ending; whereas everything started will eventually cease to actively operate; the living behavior of the thing will die and it will be dead.

All movement and action will be no more! Remember the scripture tells us that;

"Therefore if any man be in Christ, he is a new creature: old things are passed

away, *behold all things are become new.*
[II Corinthians 7:15]

The formidable word of this scripture is the word; *"in"*. Even David said that he would dwell *"in"* the house of the Lord; Paul says; If any man be; *"in"* Christ. Can you see the connection here in the scripture?

Are you in the Lord or are you at the possible idea of the Lord's existence? Just as many people are only at the church; but we see clearly that they are not yet in the church as there have been no visible change in them, that bespeak of their move from earthly to glorious in their living styles?

We are more blessed now to know when "IN" begins; as it doesn't take a rocket science to know whenever we are out?

There are so many things relative to our living experiences here on the earth that is totally impossible for us to achieve, or to make happen when being positioned on the outside of where we need to be for that which we are determined to do, to make it happen.

You would never attempt at going down the highway at a high rate of speed on the outside of your car?

You will have no control of the car and a much slimmer chance of living; you would probably die instantaneously!

The homeless, are declared to be so because they have no houses to live in, nor apartment homes to dwell in; they live out-side in the elements of the atmosphere; out-side of neighborhood dwelling with the people who have known them; and they live on the outside of what is respected and known to all of us as descent living.

What about the people who live out loud on the outside of anything that is Christian respectively on purpose; though they may even also be members of a local church somewhere, they adamantly refuse to behave themselves as one who is ruled and governed by the Holy bible?

Sadly; some people of the churches are encouraged to believe that they are living inside of salvation any way; since they had spoken words of biblical confessions even though their hearts were never involved in the matter!

"I'm "IN" the House of the Lord!"

"IN"; began the moment that I surrendered my whole body, soul, and spirit to the Lord, and allowed Him to fill me with the Holy Ghost!

The scripture speaks often in reference to "the House of"; like as of to the House of Jacob; all the

Verse ~ Six

House of Israel; the House of David; and more.

While this phrase is not at all in reference to any particular residence or place of living, it is spoken in reference to being encompassed to all of God's people included under the Domaine of the Kingdom dominion of the Lord.

I am a kingdom dweller; therefore I'm in His name; which gives deference to the fact that I am dwelling in the house of the Lord; starting now!

The name of the Lord can never and will never be erased or otherwise done away with; it is forever! It is God and only God who determines whether we are in and never out, as it related to being in the house of the Lord forever.

Doesn't matter what your doctrinal message may be to your congregation, it is what God has said in the scripture that matters relative to being in the house of the Lord; forever.

Once saved always saved; once in never out; sin is not seen as sin anymore once you have been saved; all lies from Satan. Sin is always sin, and God's total rejection of sin is eternal.

If God wanted to allow us to live like Satan even though we have claimed to be born of the spirit; Born-Again; He could have allowed Satan to be the devil in heaven, never casting him out for his outrageous iniquity!

Most people want to know the difference between sin and iniquity? Iniquity ~ In-iquity; begins with the word (in); which means that one has to be in the Lord before iniquity can be committed.

INIQUTY ~ IS WHENEVEN YOU'RE IN THE LORD; FILLED WITH THE HOLY GHOST, AND HAVE BEEN LIVING IN THE PRESENCE OF THE LORD HAVING BECOME A WORSHIPPER; YOU DECIDE TO GO AFTER SIN KNOWING THAT IT IS WRONG, BUT YOU CHOOSE TO DO IT ANYWAY! [Ezekiel 28:15]

God is not crazy or confused; sin initiated with the devil; God put the devil out of the house of the Lord; now why would God allow and permit us and any other people to live exactly like the devil and stay in the house of the Lord; and or under the power of His presence?

The fact is that many of you are out of total fellowship with God; but don't want to realize it; or acknowledge the fact that God doesn't approve of your lifestyle of sin. God does love all sinners; but He hate all sin; no exceptions!

Subjects as of this one; is very difficult for many to digest, because you have been taught that God is Love; GOD IS LOVE! But God's love is not a permit for those of us who have been submerged under-

neath the word of God; to sin like a rockstsar in a never ending party.

God loves you as you are; that being the reason that Jesus came to the earth to make us better than we are, or were.

Most people would have to admit that they are not even happy or satisfied being who they are, and they are seeking different methods to build themselves morally and spiritually and to effect change to become better than they are.

Most of the very same people don't even know and often they don't care to know who they are in the spirit; they're just ok with being commonly associated people, and that of course is their problem my friend.

On the other hand; a great percentage of the people who are at least in the churches are spiritually disgusted with themselves; but they are not motivated to fast and to pray that their spiritual lives might be enhanced and perfected for the master's use!

Perhaps they might feel that since they are not at all concerned with their lack of spiritual fortitude that God is also ok with their situation in the spirit?

God is not complaining as He overlook them to use the more dedicated people of the churches it might appear to them?

Never allow yourself to be satisfied with not hearing from the Lord; you can't allow someone else to tell you if God is pleased with you! You need to know for yourself!

Even in the day of the High Priest of the temple of God; David was assured of the fact that God was indeed please with him. He said; *I will dwell in the house of the Lord forever*; never did he say that I will stay in the temple at the altar forever.

He knew the difference between what we now refer to as the church and the ultimate truth about the house of the Lord. David knew that all of whom came under the authority and rule of the name of the Lord; would dwell in the house of the Lord; forever.

Doesn't matter where you naturally reside on the face of the planet; all of God's children can say that they are right now dwelling in the house of the Lord; and that it's forever! Good God; Thank You...

I concede to tell you that if it were never possible to be out with the Lord; as Lucifer (the now infamous Satan); was not only in the house of the Lord but already in Heaven, created as an heavenly being, for the purpose of worshipping God; leading all of the heavenly host of heaven in worshipping God; he was eternally outed as a result of iniquity being found in his heart. [Ezekiel 28:14-19]

He was created most beautiful

and was given a position irreplaceable among the entire host of heaven; thus you and I and all of the people of the earth were made for the glory of the Lord; we were put in place to replace the fallen worshipper who could never be the worshipper again.

How many have taken the time to notice that no other heavenly being had been chosen to take the place of Lucifer?

Already the position and the person of Lucifer was indeed eternal; as Lucifer lost his position in Heaven; his make as a musician having instruments and organs constructed within his body were never taken from him.

Since he wanted to exalt himself above that of God; he now has the eternal curse of his spiritual eternal self to deal with; but in time having no physical form with which to dwell in the earth.

The music that he is now responsible for reminds him of how he fouled it all up in Heaven; the music that he creates no longer have the ability to remind others to praise and to glorify God.

It is a very sad commentary that so many people are taught to never read the Old Testament of the bible; suggesting that the things of that part of the scriptures are now obsolete and insignificant to living today.

How sad it is that so many people are being denied the opportunity and the ability to see God the Father; and what Heaven on Earth could have been like?

As a result people think that they will only dwell in the house of the Lord after they will have died on the earth?

News flash for you; if you refuse to live with Lord now while you're alive and doing whatever you please, you won't be able to live with the Lord after you will have left the earth in death.

Come on church let's tell the people the truth; as many as possible; so that they will be able to live with us now and then in Heaven with the Father; Heaven was not designed for me to be there alone, I'm taking as many with me as I possibly can.

As a child in the Baptist church I use to sing a song which said; "Come and Go With Me to My Father's House" it was indeed a good song.

The composer of that song was a quite descriptive in their writing, as they spoke of things in Heaven that are sure to be found there after death; they failed however to speak of the house of the Lord in this present reality; in us!

Even though John the revelator said in Revelation; that he saw a new Heaven and a new Earth; the first heaven and the

first earth were passed away!

Even with that being so the truth of the scripture, Heaven is real and it exist now; right now! Finally; THE HOUSE OF THE LORD; IS NOW; RIGHT NOW!

Forever has already been activated in the all of the realm of the spiritually righteous; perhaps you need to catch hold of the reality of right now, because there is no such thing as being able to catch up in the spirit realm.

It would be most empowering for you to begin confessing to yourself right now; "I'm In the House of the Lord; Foerever!"

"Comentary on The 23rd Psalms"

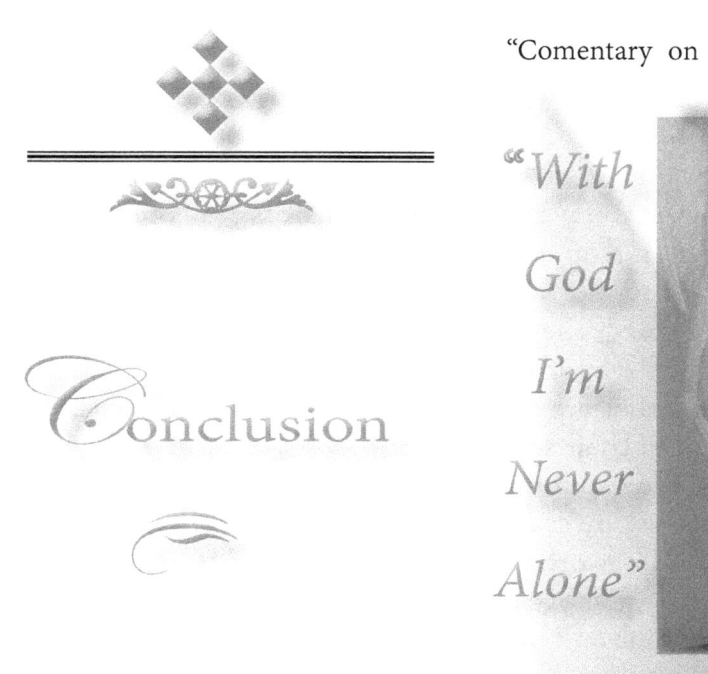

Psalms 23; Conclusion

Let us hear the conclusion of the whole matter: Fear God; and keep his commandments: for this is the whole duty of man. For God shall bring every work into judgement, with every secret thing, whether it be good, or whether it be evil. [Ecclesiastes 12:13-14]

"Now That You Have Looked With Me"

Finally; this is the revealed understanding of the scripture, as it was given to me. I did not write the bible and neither did anyone else on the face of the planet that is alive right now. The bible was here when we all got here; and it doesn't matter that so many people feel that their lives would be better lived without the authority of the scripture; the word of God stands!

As it relates to the word of God; the struggle that most people have is Jesus Christ! Truly believing in Jesus Christ requires a dedicated change and a commitment to follow after the instruction of the scripture for a life of holiness and of righteousness.

My last book; "Captured; Comprehensive; and Defined"; I purposefully made the statement that you will never find anything that

you are not willing to look for. Some things in this life that you determine that you really desire that are not readily accessible for you to have the possession of, you must certainly go and search vigorously for them.

Most assuredly the greatest reward of searching for anything is finding exactly what you were searching for. Lots of people look for things, but are often stopped just short of finding it; on the other hand there is a greater portion of the people who when determined to find a certain thing, they are not going to stop until they find it; no matter what; even if the ultimate find of the search reveals that the thing that they are looking for doesn't exist; they are driven unto the very end of their search!

Sometimes we are searching for our own benefit, and then there are the times that we are searching and digging deeply for the benefit of others. God has ordained that there would be those people in the kingdom who make ready the prepared meal for the kingdom dwellers to richly dine and be fed sufficiently.

The Lord spoke to me and said; for centuries now many people have been satisfied with what someone else determined the word of God to be saying, whether it was the truth or error; fact is that some people just literally miss the meaning and the understanding of the meaning! They were just okay with being told exactly what to believe, making it easier for them to exist in any denominational atmosphere.

Hearing this in my spirit, brought ease and a sense of conformation that I had indeed done the will of God in delivering this message to the people. My moto that preaching is not at all about how many handshakes and pats you get on the back or relative to the number of people who purport to have been blessed by your message; rather it is all about knowing that you have said exactly what the Lord has instructed for you to say!

I took an issue with the wording of the New American Standard; revised version of the King James bible; it reads to me as if God is being portrayed as the new Santa Clause ~ Slot Machine; even of the most awesome gospel recording choir back in the eighties; recorded and released the song saying; "Because the Lord is my shepherd; I have everything I need"; and so on...

I played the song for many choirs cringing all of the time because

Conclusion

the song just didn't set well in my spirit because I know that God; is God! He's the master of the universe; just as we don't tell God when to allow the darkness to fall on the night, and the sunlight of shine on the day; we don't tell God when how or where to bless us.

I begin to hear down in my own spirit that the people of the churches who confess salvation and to being filled with the Holy Ghost; that they are deceitfully being led astray, whereas they don't want to follow God of the King James bible any more, and that they are tired of suffering for any reason; they have determined that they are not going through anything that test them or tries their ideas of faith?

They are now saying; "Since you are God; just give me whatever I want without all of that, you know me; it doesn't take all of that just to get blessing from you."

I would visit other churches and the same scriptural representation coming across the pulpit during the sermon from the minister or maybe a deacon or someone who is supposed to be inspired to share with the people in that congregation, that it doesn't take all of that to please the Lord; go get your blessing; would be spoken. I'm saying within myself; wait a minute; that's not what the bible says!

Then of course to have conversation with different people who think of themselves to be very spiritual and biblical astute; during our conversation they would reach back and pull the 23rd Psalm from their memory, and begin butchering the meaning of the message all over again just as so many others had done; simply based on what they had indeed been taught.

Sometimes I made the attempt to try to share the revelation with them that the Lord had indeed spoken to me concerning the 23rd Psalms, but because they were so indoctrinated they could not hear me. The scripture says on many occasions; "he that hath an ear to hear; let him hear what the spirit have to say unto the church!" That is indication that everybody listening is not going to hear; doesn't matter who the messenger is!

It is very important for us who preach the word of God to be well studied and well versed of the scripture because you are going to be the first minister to deliver a certain message; whether you are right or indeed in error to the scripture; some of those people are going to be dead set on the fact that you said it that way, and they

will refuse to turn away from the message that you brought. Your charismatic flash and flair can often have a permanently binding effect on the minds of some people; think about that while being so proud that the people heard from you.

We need desperately to come together and to teach the word of God with pin point accuracy according to the written word of the scripture; I read and study from the King James Bible. Time is shorter than whenever we first believed; there is no more time to argue the scriptures and to debate our denominations; the Kingdom of God is at hand and swiftly moving into place for the imminent return of the Lord Jesus Christ! Oh yes He's coming soon! Fall into place with the Lord and fall in Love with the Love of God; do all that is within you to be impacting to the people who are around you on a consistent basis.

I may be a bit different, but not near as skeptical and distrusting as many others may be indeed; but I have not become one who go along with everybody just because they agree with a particular method or teaching of the scripture.

Whenever I get a check in my spirit that something is off or even that something is missing or going in the wrong direction, I am individual enough to stop and examine what is going on with me or around me. The spirit of the Lord; The Holy Ghost will check you and alert you to Look Again; even though the messenger may be vowing that what they are saying is the truth!

Whatever the spirit of the Lord says is right; and He's right the first time!

God will never speak or go against His own word; you will find that whatever the Lord is saying will be in accordance to His written word and extremely accurate to the immediate surrounding atmosphere that you are presently in. God does not bless mess; and neither has he blessed the mis-interpreted mess of this 23rd Psalms.

God has not shown pity on the people who have believed in the slanted message which had been purposefully misguided in the wrong direction. Don't believe for one moment that God said well I feel sorry for the people who have been deceived and taught erroneously concerning the scripture; so I'll just bless them anyway?

NO! God wants you to know the truth and to abide by the truth! Every operation of faith must be according to the written word of

Conclusion

God, in effort to move the Father in Heaven to answer our prayers and to honor our prayerful request. God even wants you to come to Him in spirit and in truth;[St. John 4:24] so how do you approach God bearing the truth of God's word now turned into a lie?

You can't just look at God and say to Him; well you know what I mean; you're God and you know your own word, I might not be saying it right but it's in your bible?

That's a sad example of a person who is supposed to believe what the bible says so to the point that they will even take the word of the bible back to God who gave us the bible to believe in the first place. You want God to know that you believe His word; don't try to take it back to Him all jumbled up and misconstrued; words of the scripture left out omitted or replaced with words of much less substance and authority.

It's like having a pregnant mother in the hospital who is in labor, ready to give birth to her child; but after giving birth to her baby, a dead baby of another nationality is brought to her and it is said to be her baby that she had just given birth to? People grammatically kill and literally destroy the written word of God, but expect for God to be honorable to these now unrecognizable sentences; when it's not even what He said, and certainly never what He meant!

The mother is expecting an alive; breathing child full of life and activity as an infant child would be full of life and living; crying to the top of its lungs for its mother, perhaps wanting to fed. But instead what has been brought to her is a dead corpse not even of the same bloodline and national race as she is; it's a stranger's baby!

The mother doesn't desire the baby and the babe can't even desire this, the wrong mother, because there is no life in it. As this picture parable comes in clearer to you; so it is with the word of God, and the carrier who brings the word back to the Lord in prayer.

God can't even react to the error that has been brought back to Him, as there is no life nor living activity in the word. The word reacts to God whenever it is presented to Him, as God reacts in thorough excitement and faith-filled activity; as He the Lord is faithful. My friend; GOD KNOWS HIS WORD! Taking erroneous scripture to the Lord aborts your prayer, and it will kill any request that you may have of the Lord.

The people of the past generation teachers and preachers; who

were taught to see God only as this great giver and provider to them, all it was that they would have to do was to name it and claim it; so many of the people have fallen away haven had their prayer request nullified and left unfulfilled. Those same people want to convince others not to believe that bible because it doesn't work; when all along the problem and the failure was in the fact that they had been taught and wrongfully instructed to believe that God could be prayerfully push around; and scripturally bullied!

I grew up in the church where we sang the song which says; *"Anyway You Bless Me I'll Be Satisfied!"*

We as people will have a tendency to ask God for things that we are not even ready for; we are not even capable of handling those things that would totally take us away from God; and totally out of the faith in God? I preached a message back in 2005 titled; "What If God Gives You Everything That You Want?"

What need would you really have for God; knowing that everything that you needed God for had already been given to you? How would you handle praying to God if you could simply tell God what you wanted from Him and get what you want from Him, alike a genie in a bottle; even though your desires were against the word and the will of God for your life? How could the Lord; our God; ever mean anything to you, if there was never any testing or trials to build the relationship that you need in an effort to know him?

> *That I may know him, and the power of His resurrection, and the fellowship of his sufferings, being made conformable unto his death. Brethren I count not myself to have apprehended: but this one thing I do, forgetting those things which are behind, and reaching forth of those things which are before, I press towards the mark for the prize of the high calling of God in Christ Jesus.* [Philippians 3:10; 13-14;]

God works in many different ways to get you to come to a place of growth and maturity in Him and in His word, so that you will be an excellent witness, able to convince the sinner of their sins, and that they need to turn to the Lord and be saved, but also to be led of the Lord on a daily basis. Without leaning to the Lord, you don't have anything to show to them that will ask of you, that the Lord is your shepherd; and that as a result you really don't have anything to worry about.

Conclusion

God has all power and authority; but make no mistake, it's God's power and authority! God said to Job; I will ask a question; you answer if you are able to do so! [Paraphrasing; Job chapters 38, 39, 40 & 41;]

Job; who loved God; incomparable to any man of his surrounding in all the land of Uz', which God testified of this truth to Satan; Job wanted to call God into question about the trials that he had gone through. You know whenever we feel that we are living all that we are required to live for God; we seem to want to hold God to a standard which excludes us from all misfortunes and disappointments.

This sickened society of church people who have been blessed to experience this new millennium; they are now bringing the church and all that is indeed of God into question for the penalties of their own sinful behavior and their bad choices of living? They are determined that they are not going to have any experiences like Job had? These twisted people have become apologetic to Satan and to the sinners of the world who have chosen sin as their lifestyle; and they do not see the need for turning to the Lord to be changed. They behave themselves nowadays as if to suggest that it's God's problem that He can't deal with their sins; not their problem?

It sort of makes you sick to the stomach to hear the sinners of today talk about the bible and the people of the church and even of God in Jesus Christ. God is able to take the very breath that you are breathing right now, and He is God enough to take everything that is alive concerning you right out of the very day that you are standing in right now!

God could do to you everything that hell is going to do to you at any moment; but God would rather that you come to repentance and change your ways. God is not at all interested in you knowing the power of His wrath from the standpoint of being the one in trouble needing to be chastised for the wrong that you know you are doing in your life that is contrary to the word of God.

> The Lord is not slack concerning his promise, as some men count slackness; but is longsuffering to us-ward, not willing that any should perish but that all should come to repentance. But the day of the Lord shall come as a thief in the night, in the which the heavens shall pass away with great noise, and the elements shall melt away with fervent heat, the earth also and the works that are therein shall be burned up. Seeing that all these things shall be dissolved, what man-

ner of persons ought ye to be in all holy conversations and godliness, looking for and hasting for the coming of the day of God, wherein the heavens being on fire shall be dissolved, and the elements shall melt with fervent heat? Nevertheless we, according to his promise, look for new heavens and new earth, wherein dwelleth righteousness. Wherefore, beloved, seeing the ye look for such things, be diligent that ye may be found in his of peace, without spot and blameless. And account that the longsuffering of our Lord is salvation; even as our beloved brother Paul also according to the wisdom given unto him hath written unto you; As also in his epistles , speaking in them of these things; in which are some things hard to be understood, which they that are unlearned and unstable wrest as they do also the other scriptures, unto their own destruction. Ye therefore, beloved, seeing that ye know these things, before, beware lest ye also, being led away with the error of the wicked, fall from your own steadfastness. But grow in grace, and in the knowledge of our Lord and savior Jesus Christ. To him be glory both now and forever. Amen.   [II Peter 3:9-18]

The bible is not and will not be changing to accommodate lifestyles of sin and of self; it is to your own destruction to go ahead and to live the way that you want to disregarding the word of the Lord. God loves you and He has proven His love over and over again; He has even proven that He is God and that there is none like Him; get with God now! All that needed to be proven has already been done; Jesus Is Lord!

I urge you and I even encourage you to go back through this commentary again to reexamine the truths written here and see it for yourself; Look Again……………………………………….

Conclusion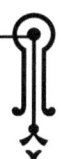

Commentary on the 23rd Psalms
by: William Thompson Jr ~ 2016

Notes : _____

Notes : _____

Notes :

Notes :

Notes : _____

Notes :

Other Topics Written and Published by WET Publishing Company:

 =============================

Available topics @ Amazon.com & Barnes&Noble.com

Word Up; It's Got To Come Out Of Your Mouth (c) 2001/2006

Just Let Jesus Do It For You   (c)2002/2007

Shepherd Wars & Sheep Attacks   Copyright 2007/2008

Once Bitten ForEver; Tree of Knowledge of Good and Evil (c)2009

Hidden N' The Light (c)2009

Captured, Comprehenive, and Defined (c)2012

Write Everlasting Tips, Publishing Company;
~ 2016 ~
is dedicated to faithfully continue penning the revealed truths from the Lord; Publishing the Excellence of God's Word ~

William Thompson, Jr. Publisher / Author...

> To submit manuscripts for publishing -
> write to WET Publishing, Co.
> 7525 Arbor Hill Dr. Fort Worth, Tx 76120
> or contact us ~ 777imgood@gmail.com

"May the Lord God Bless You; Real Good"

www.ingramcontent.com/pod-product-compliance
Lightning Source LLC
Chambersburg PA
CBHW050552300426
44112CB00013B/1881